Reconstructing
Late Pleistocene Human Behavior
in the Jordan Rift Valley

The Middle Paleolithic stone tool assemblage from Ar Rasfa

Ghufran Sabri Ahmad

John J. Shea

BAR International Series 2042

2009

Published in 2016 by
BAR Publishing, Oxford

BAR International Series 2042

Reconstructing Late Pleistocene Human Behavior in the Jordan Rift Valley

ISBN 978 1 4073 0618 6

BAR Publishing is the trading name of British Archaeological Reports (Oxford) Ltd.
British Archaeological Reports was first incorporated in 1974 to publish the BAR
Series, International and British. In 1992 Hadrian Books Ltd became part of the BAR
group. This volume was originally published by Archaeopress in conjunction with
British Archaeological Reports (Oxford) Ltd / Hadrian Books Ltd, the Series principal
publisher, in 2009. This present volume is published by BAR Publishing, 2016.

Printed in England

BAR
PUBLISHING

BAR titles are available from:

BAR Publishing
122 Banbury Rd, Oxford, OX2 7BP, UK
EMAIL   info@barpublishing.com
PHONE   +44 (0)1865 310431
FAX   +44 (0)1865 316916
www.barpublishing.com

ABSTRACT

RECONSTRUCTING LATE PLEISTOCENE HUMAN BEHAVIOR IN THE JORDAN RIFT VALLEY: THE
MIDDLE PALEOLITHIC STONE TOOL ASSEMBLAGE FROM AR RASFA

Ghufran Sabri Ahmad and John J. Shea

Ar Rasfa is a Middle Paleolithic open-air site located in the Rift Valley of Northwest Jordan excavated between 1997-1999. This book presents a detailed technological, typological, and paleoanthropological analysis of the stone tool assemblage from Ar Rasfa. Artifacts reflecting the initial preparation and exploitation of local flint sourcse dominate the Ar Rasfa assemblage. Typologically, the assemblage is most similar to Levantine Mousterian assemblages such as those from Naamé, Skhul and Qafzeh. Patterns of lithic variability and contextual evidence suggest Ar Rasfa was visited intermittently by human populations circulating between lake/river-edge resources in the Rift Valley bottom and woodland habitats along the ridge of the Transjordan Plateau.

TABLE OF CONTENTS

LIST OF FIGURES

LIST OF TABLES

PREFACE

This book grew out of Ghufan Ahmad's Master's Thesis research in the Department of Anthropology at Stony Brook University between 2008-2009. We thank Professor Donny Youkhanna and Professor Katheryn Twiss for their insightful comments on earlier drafts of this manuscript. We also thank Patricia Crawford, Ph.D., for proofreading and general advice.

The excavation of the Ar Rasfa site was funded by grants (to Shea) by the L.S.B. Leakey Foundation and the American Schools of Oriental Research. He is thankful for the logistical support provided in Jordan by the Ministry of Antiquities and Tourism and by the American Center for Oriental Research in Amman. Shea further thanks Mr. Yacoub Maryoud Oweis of the Ajlun Office of the Ministry of Antiquities for his outstanding service as Antiquities Representative at Ar Rasfa in 1997 and 1999.

Gufran Ahmad's research was funded by a grant (to Professor Elizabeth Stone) by the Andrew Mellon Foundation. Ahmad also expresses his sincere thanks to Prof. Stone, to the staff of the Graduate School of Stony Brook University, to his fellow Stony Brook graduate students, and to his colleaguues and Mosul University and the Ministry of Higher Education of Iraq.

CHAPTER 1.

INTRODUCTION

The earliest and latest phases of the Paleolithic differ dramatically from one another. Even the earliest prehistorians had little difficulty interpreting Upper Paleolithic artifacts in terms of similar items in recent human hunter-gatherer material culture. The Lower Paleolithic is strikingly different in all respects. No recently-living human society creates an archaeological record even remotely similar to the Lower Paleolithic.

The Lower Paleolithic Period began in Africa 2,500,000 years ago (2.5 Mya) and witnessed the appearance of many hominin species, such as *Homo habilis*, *H. ergaster/erectus* and *H. heidelbergensis* (Klein 2009). These hominins lived in Africa and Southern Asia, mainly in warm and humid tropical habitats (Antón and Swisher 2004, Dennell 2009). They used simple technology to make pebble cores, flake tools and handaxes (Shea 2007a). These stone tools are thought to have been used while held directly in the hand and not attached to wooden handles. Preserved heavy wooden spears like those found at Schöningen, Lehringen, and other European Middle Pleistocene sites (Theime 1997) are the only evidence of hunting weapons. Lower Paleolithic hominin diet undoubtedly varied widely over time and space (see papers in Ungar 2007). The most labor-intensive foods, protein and fat from larger mammal prey, were probably obtained by mixed strategies of scavenging and hunting (Domínguez-Rodrigo and Pickering 2003). There is no evidence of systematic trade and exchange networks, prolonged site occupation and architecture, or of the use of artifacts as symbols (Chase 1991, Gamble 1999, 2007, Kuhn and Stiner 2001). The end of the Lower Paleolithic Period is generally dated ca. 200,000-250,000 years ago (200-250 Kya)(Dibble and McPherron 2007, Monnier 2007).

The Upper Paleolithic Period (45-10 Kya) witnessed the permanent dispersal of anatomically modern humans (*Homo sapiens*) in Eurasia (Richard G. Klein 2008, Trinkaus 2005). They are the only hominin species associated with Upper Paleolithic assemblages (Klein 2009, Mellars 2005). Geographically, Upper Paleolithic humans and their contemporaries occupied all of Africa and all but the most northern latitudes of Eurasia (Brantingham et al. 2001, Hoffecker 2004). These humans lived in both warm humid climates and cold, dry ones (Foley 1987). Upper Paleolithic tool technology became more complex than in any previous period, incorporating carved bone, antler, stone, and other materials that were not extensively used by earlier hominins (Mellars 1994). Small hafted stone tools, projectile weapons and blades were also common elements of the Upper Paleolithic period (Knecht 1994, Kuhn and Stiner 2001, Shea 2006c). Systematic hunting, fishing, and the exploitation of smaller prey species are clearly evident in ways that are only ambiguously demonstrable for Lower Paleolithic contexts (Richards et al. 2005, Stiner 1993). Upper Paleolithic people conducted long-distance trade and exchange, and they settled for prolonged periods at the same sites (Gamble 1999). They made extensive use of fire, not just for light/heat, but also for cooking, bone-degreasing, and for the production of fired ceramic figurines (Marean 2007, Soffer 2001). European sites contain clear evidence for freestanding architecture and plausible evidence for watercraft (Soffer 1985, 2004). Upper Paleolithic humans also created a rich array of symbolic artifacts, including decorated tools, musical instruments, mineral pigments, personal adornments and both abstract and representational art (Bahn and Vertut 1997, Guthrie 2005).

In formulating explanations for the differences between Lower and Upper Paleolithic Periods, archaeologists have often focused on the Middle Paleolithic Period (245-45 Kya) (Klein 2008, Trinkaus 2005). This period witnessed the origin of *Homo sapiens* and the emergence of our species' distinctive behaviors (d'Errico 2003, Foley and Lahr 1997, Klein 2008, McBrearty 2007, McBrearty and Brooks 2000, Shea et al. 2007, White et al. 2003). Searching for the origins of *Homo sapiens*' Upper Paleolithic behavior in local Middle Paleolithic contexts can be problematical. In Europe and western Asia, Middle Paleolithic assemblages are associated mainly with Neandertals (*Homo neanderthalensis*). The Middle Paleolithic record for Southwest Asia is even more complex. There, both Neandertals and *Homo sapiens* are found with similar evidence and in roughly contemporaneous contexts (Bar-

Table 1.1 Excavated Levantine Middle Paleolithic Sites.

Region and Sites	Cave Open-Air?	Radiometric Dates (Kya) and Method	Principal References.
Lebanon and coastal Syria			
Naame	open-air	90±20 (US)	Fleisch (1970)
Ksar Akil	cave	47±9 (US) 44±3.7 (^{14}C)	Marks and Volkman(1986)
Keoue	cave		Nishiaki and Copeland (1992)
Bezez	cave		Copeland (1983)
Nahr Ibrahim	cave	78±24 (ESR)	Solecki (1970)
Ras el-Kelb	cave		Copeland (1998)
Interior Syria			
Yabrud	cave	115±17 - 139±21 (ESR)	Rust (1950), Solecki and Solecki (1995)
Douara	cave	75 (FT)	Akazawa and Sakaguchi (1987)
Jerf Ajla	cave	33.3±2.3 (TL) 42.5±2.5 (^{14}C)	Coon (1957), Schroeder (1969)
Dederiyeh	cave		Akazawa, et al. (2003)
Umm el Tlel	open-air	36±2.5 (TL) 34.5±0.8 (^{14}C)	Boëda and Muhesen (1993)
Hummal 1		128±9 (TL)	Le Tensorer (2004)
Biqat Quneitra	open-air	39-54 (ESR)	Goren-Inbar (1990)
North-Central Israel & Palestine National Authority			
Hayonim	cave	150-200 (TL) 164-241 (ESR)	Meignen (1998)
Tabun	cave	165-245 (TL) 76-203 (ESR) 51-110 (US)	Garrod (1937a), Jelinek (1982a)
Tirat Carmel	open-air		Ronen (1974)
Qafzeh	cave	92±5 (TL) 96-110 (ESR)	Hovers (2009)
Amud	cave	58-69 (TL) 53-70 (US)	Hovers (2004)
Skhul	cave	119 (TL) 76-101 (ESR) 49 (US)	McCown (1937)
El Wad	cave		Garrod (1937b)
Shovakh	cave		Binford (1966)
Kebara	cave	52-62 (TL) 61-64 (ESR)	Bar-Yosef and Meignen (2008)
Sefunim	cave		Ronen (1984)
Misliya	cave		Weinstein-Evron, et al. (2003)
Zuttiyeh	cave	106-157 (TL)	Turville-Petre (1927), Gisis and Bar-Yosef(1974)
Geulah	cave	45 (^{14}C)	Wreschner (1967)
Shukhbah	cave		Callander (2004)
West Bank/Judean Desert			
Abu Sif			Neuville (1934)
Tabban	cave		Neuville (1934)
Sahba	cave		Neuville (1934)
Larikba	unknown?		Vandermeersch (1966)
Erq el-Ahmar	cave		Neuville (1934), Phillips and Saca (2002)
Northern Jordan			
Ar-Rasfa	open-air		Shea (1999a)
Negev/Sinai			
Ein Aqev	open-air		Munday (1976)
Rosh Ein Mor	open-air	200 (US)	Crew (1976)
Farah II	open-air	49-62 (ESR)	Gilead and Grigson (1984)
Southern Jordan			
Tor Faraj	cave	48 (TL)	Henry (1995b, 2003)

Region and Sites	Cave Open-Air?	Radiometric Dates (Kya) and Method	Principal References.
Tor Sabiha	cave	32 (US) 69 (AAR)	Henry (1995b)
Ain Difla	cave		Clark, et al. (1997)

NOTE: For complete listing of dates and references, see Shea (2003b, 2008). Dating method abbreviations: AAR = Amino acid racemization, ESR = Electron-spin resonance, FT = Fission-track, TL = Thermoluminescence, US = Uranium-series, [14]C= radiocarbon.

Yosef 2000, Bar-Yosef and Vandermeersch 1993, Shea 2003a, Shea 2003b).

The "Levant" is defined as the region that stretches from the Taurus-Zagros Mountains of Anatolia south to the Sinai Peninsula along the eastern coast of the Mediterranean Sea (Blondel and Aronson 1999). Ecologically, the Levant includes areas adjacent to the seacoast covered by Mediterranean (oak-terebinth) woodland and Irano-Turanian steppe ecozones (Zohary 1973). Currently, the climate of the Levant features hot dry summers and cool humid winters (Zohary 1973). The Levant's Late Pleistocene climate was colder and drier than the present but punctuated by intervals of warm and humid conditions (MIS 5e, 5a) (Almogi-Labin et al. 2004, Goldberg 1995).

Many Middle Paleolithic archeological sites have been found in the Levant in contexts dating to between 245-45 Kya BP (for a recent overview, see Shea 2003b)(See Figure 1.1). The most recently excavated Levantine Middle Paleolithic sites are Dederiyeh Cave, Umm el Tel, Tabun Cave, Amud Cave, Qafzeh Cave, Kebara Cave, Hayonim Cave, Biqat Quneitra, and Tor Faraj Rockshelter (see Table 1.1). These sites are distributed in southern Turkey, Sinai, Jordan, Palestine (West Bank), Israel, Syria, and Lebanon. Of the better-documented sites listed in Table 1, 30/39 or 76% are caves or rockshelters. Most of these Middle Paleolithic sites are located in northern Israel (Mt. Carmel and the Galilee). The region with the fewest documented Middle Paleolithic sites is Northern Jordan. Only a small number of Levantine Middle Paleolithic contexts have been dated by geochronometric techniques. The majority of dates for Levantine Middle Paleolithic contexts fall in early part of the Late Pleistocene, 130-45 Kya BP, or Marine Isotope Stages 5-4 (MIS 5-4).

In biogeographic terms, the Levant encompasses a transition zone between the Palearctic (Europe and Western Asia), Paleo-tropical (southern Asia) and the Ethiopian (north African) faunal realms (Tchernov 1988). Animal species from all three of these biogeographic realms are represented among faunal evidence from Levantine Middle Paleolithic sites. Palearctic species are most ubiquitous and usually most common (as numbered by NISP) (Stiner 2006). These species include mountain gazelle, wild boar, ibex, and fallow deer. The particular species found and their relative abundance varies from site to site, probably reflecting local ecological conditions (Tchernov 1998). For example, camel and steppe ass are rare among coastal sites, but common at more arid sites in Syria.

Hominin fossils from Levantine Middle Paleolithic contexts belong to two species, Neandertals (*Homo neanderthalensis*) and early *Homo sapiens* (Hublin 2000). Levantine Neandertals and early *Homo sapiens* differ morphologically both from each other, and from other Neandertal and *Homo sapiens* populations (Kramer et al. 2001). The genetic and evolutionary relationships between Levantine Neandertals and *Homo sapiens* and between Levantine Middle Paleolithic hominins and those from other regions have been the subject of much speculation (Binford 1968, Binford 1970, Brose and Wolpoff 1970, Howell 1958, Howell 1959, Hublin 2000, Wolpoff 1989). There is currently no evidence for prolonged occupation of the same part of the Levant by Neandertals and *Homo sapiens* at the same time (Clark and Lindly 1988, cf. Hovers 2006, Shea 2007c, 2008).

Stone tools from Levantine Middle Paleolithic sites are assigned to the "Levantine Mousterian" Industry. This industry shares many of the same artifact types and techniques seen at other Middle Paleolithic sites in West Asia, Europe and North Africa. Levantine Mousterian assemblages differ from those in neighboring regions in that they show more frequent use of laminar Levallois core technology to produce triangular and sub-triangular flakes (Meignen 1988). Many Levantine Mousterian assemblages also feature truncated-and-facetted-pieces (cores on flakes) used to make small flakes (Hovers 2007). Levantine Mousterian assemblages lack heavily retouched scrapers and bifaces (handaxes and foliate points) like those found in Eurasian and North African Mousterian assemblages (Dibble 1991, Shea 2003b).

Most overviews of Levantine Middle Paleolithic industrial variability assign "Levantine Mousterian" assemblages to one of three different chronologically successive groups (Bar-Yosef 2000, Copeland 1975, Jelinek 1982a, Ronen 1979, Shea 2001, Shea 2003b). The principal technological and typological differences among these assemblage-groups are listed in Table 5.1. Early Levantine Mousterian assemblages generally date to before the Last Interglacial during MIS 6-7, ca. 130-245 Kya. Middle Levantine Mousterian assemblages date to the Last Interglacial (broadly defined) or MIS 5. Later Levantine Mousterian assemblages consistently date to the initial stages of the main Würm Glaciation, 47-75 Kya, or MIS 4-early MIS 3. For descriptive and comparative purposes, this study employs the chronostratigraphic framework for Levantine Middle Paleolithic variability recently proposed by Shea (2001, 2003b)(see Table 1.2).

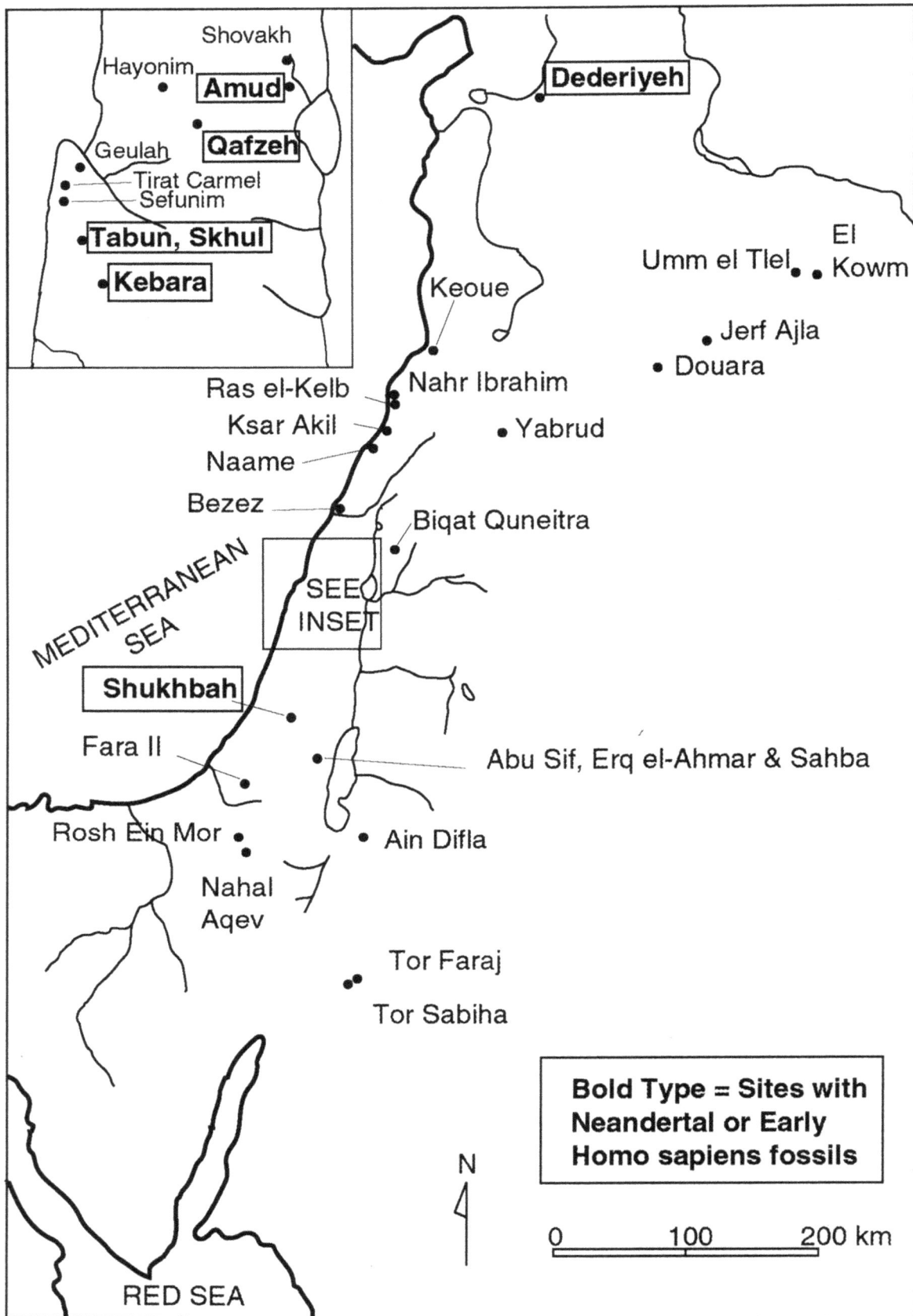

Figure 1.1 Map of Levant showing important Middle Paleolithic sites (modified from Shea 2003b, used with permission).

Table 1.2 Frameworks of Levantine Mousterian Industrial Variability (Modified after Shea (2001: Table 3)).

Phase & Dates	Cores Technology	Flake Tool Typology	Representative Assemblages
Early Levantine Mousterian 245-130 Kya	Recurrent Levallois cores with unidirectional-parallel and bidirectional-parallel preparation. Many elongated blanks with Minimal striking platform preparation.	Blanks: Elongated flakes, blades, and points. Retouched tools: Numerous Upper Paleolithic types (endscrapers burins, perforators, backed knives).	Tabun Units II-IX Abu Sif B-C Rosh Ein Mor Nahal Aqev 3 Hayonim lower E-F 'Ain Difla (WHS 634) Douara IV Ksar Akil XXVIII
Middle Levantine Mousterian 130-75 Kya	Recurrent Levallois cores with radial/centripetal preparation. Numerous discoidal cores and cores-on-flakes.	Blanks: Large oval Levallois flakes, and pseudo-Levallois flakes, short Levallois points (usually few in number). Retouched tools: Numerous Middle Paleolithic types (sidescrapers, denticulates).	Tabun Unit I, beds 18-26 Naamé Skhul B Qafzeh L, XVII-XXIV Nahr Ibrahim Ras el-Kelb Ksar Akil XXVI-XXVII
Later Levantine Mousterian 75-45 Kya	Recurrent Levallois cores with unidirectional-convergent preparation. Some increased use of radial/centripetal preparation in younger levels.	Blanks: Short and broad Levallois points, Levallois blades, naturally-backed knives. Retouched tools: Numerous Middle Paleolithic types (sidescrapers, denticulates).	Tabun Unit I, beds 1-17? Kebara F, IV-XII Amud B Keoue Dederiyeh Qafzeh 12-13, L, I-XV Shukbah D Tor Faraj, Tor Sabiha Umm el Tlel V 1 (V 2(a) Shovakh I-IV Sefunim 12-13

Middle Paleolithic Sites in Jordan

More than one hundred Middle Paleolithic archeological sites are known in Jordan (Henry 1998). Most of these sites have been discovered recently (i.e., within the last twenty years), and they are known mainly from surface collections made in the course of systematic survey. Excavated and well-documented Middle Paleolithic sites are far fewer in number, but they occur throughout the country (see Figure 1.2). Most are located in southern Jordan (i.e., Jordan south of Amman, or south of 32°N latitude).

Southern Jordan has a combination of limestone and sandstone substrates, both of which are covered by extensive loess and sand deposits (Bender 1974). Deposits of *terra rosa* soils are restricted to the flanks of the Rift Valley and the Madaba Plain. Today much of southern Jordan is desertic, but numeous lines of paleoclimatic evidence suggests it was woodland-steppe when it was occupied by Middle Paleolithic humans (Henry 2003). There is little evidence for sustained Middle Paleolithic occupation of desert habitats, as there appears to be from sites in Syria (Umm el Tlel, Dederiyeh, and Douara) (Akazawa 1987, Boëda et al. 1998, Le Tensorer et al. 2007).

The southernmost Jordanian Middle Paleolithic sites are located along the Jordan- Saudi Arabia border. These are surface localities near Al Mudawwara, where "Levallois-Mousterian" artifacts overlie fossil lake beds dating to 76.8 ± 8.2 Kya and 116 ± 5.3 (by U/Th)(Abed et al. 2000).

Slightly further north and to the west in the Himsa Basin (northeast of Aqaba) teams led by Henry have investigated two Middle Paleolithic rockshelters, Tor Faraj and Tor

Sabiha (Henry 1995b, 2003). Both of these sites preserve Late Mousterian assemblages dating to around 65 Kya BP.

In the Wadi Hasa, the Ain Difla rock shelter (WHS 631) preserves an Early Mousterian assemblage together with sparse vertebrate fossil remains. These occupations have been dated to 105±15 (by TL) and 103±13/162 ±22 (ESR EU/LU) (Clark et al. 1997, Lindly and Clark 1987).

North of Aqaba, in Wadi Araba (more specifically Wadi Gharandal) recent surveys identified two Middle Paleolithic open-air sites, J603 and J602 (Henry 1982).

Surveys in the Wadi Al Koum region southwest of Amman have reported Middle Paleolithic artifacts of indeterminate age and typological affinity (Cordova et al. 2004).

In eastern Jordan, Middle Paleolithic artifacts are known from surface exposures around the el Jafr (Quintero et al. 2004) and in the Azraq Oasis (Copeland 1988, Rollefson et al. 1997).

Northwestern Jordan, which we define as Jordan north and west of Amman (north of 31° 30' N latitude, west of 36°31' E latitude) differs climatically from southern Jordan. Elevations are lower than 900 m, and rainfall is common throughout the winter months. Northwest Jordan is predominantly limestone bedrock covered with *terra rosa* soils (Bender 1974). Together with the Rift Valley bottom, the northwestern region accounts for much of Jordan's present-day agricultural productivity. Although agriculture and pastoralism have reduced the extent of original woodland, the region has tremendous potential to sustain plant and animal life. This region has a rich archaeological

5

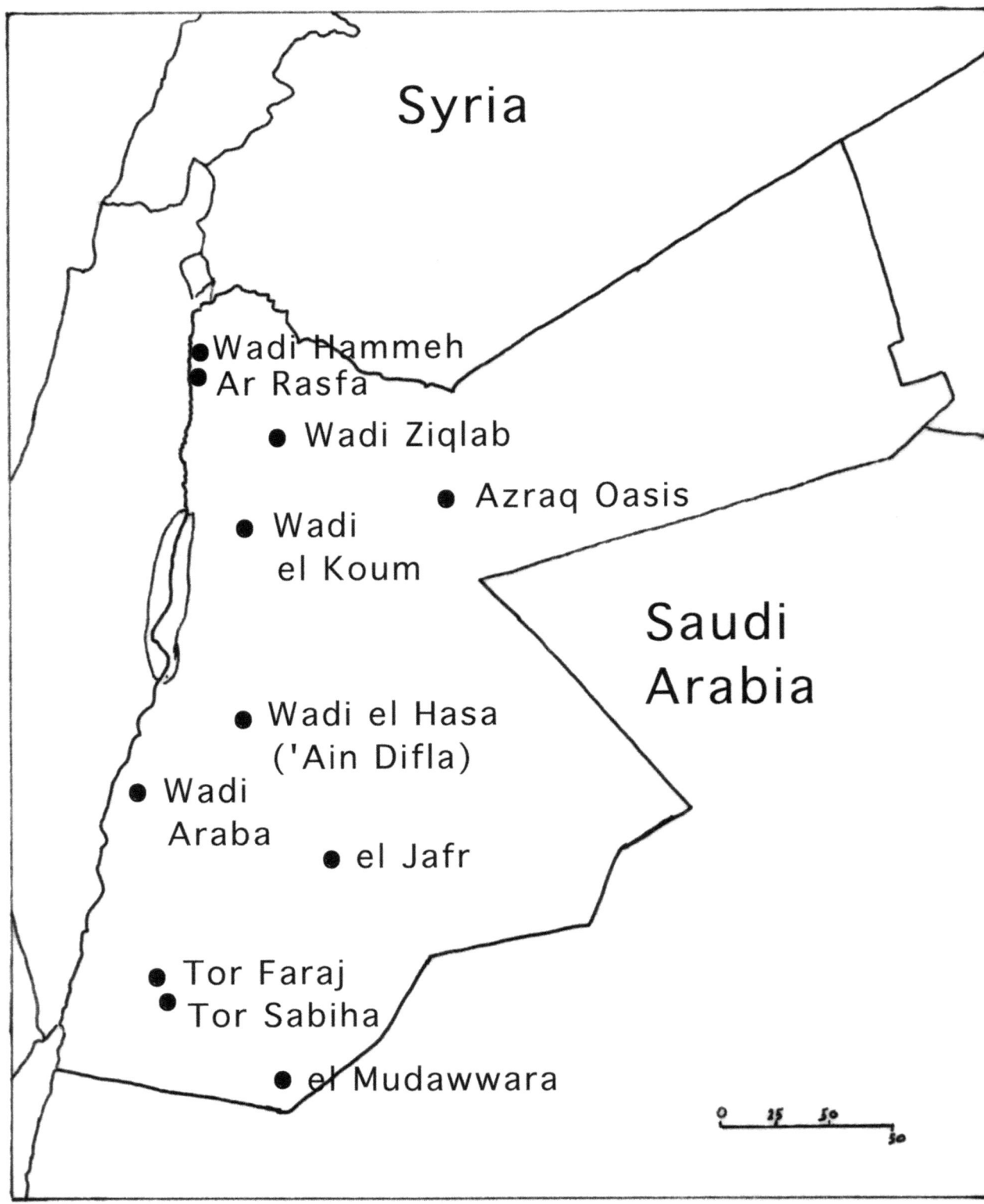

Figure 1.2 Map of Jordan showing Middle Paleolithic sites mentioned in the text.

record for recent periods (e.g., Pella, Jerash, Umm Qais), but its Middle Paleolithic record is less well documented than that of southern Jordan. Early survey of the region by Muheisen (1988) identified numerous cave and open-air sites along the Ghawr (low elevations adjacent to the Rift Valley bottom). More recent research has focused on the wadis flowing into the Jordan Valley.

Middle Paleolithic sites have been found in Wadi al Hammah at Tabaqat Fahl (Macumber 1992). These artifacts occur in numerous localities in the Late Pleistocene Abu Habil Formation.

Surveys of the Wadi Ziqlab have identified numerous

Middle Paleolithic surface sites (Banning and Fawcett 1983), but none has thus far been the subject of excavation.

Survey of the Wadi Yabis by Palumbo and colleagues (Palumbo et al. 1990) identified several open-air Middle Paleolithic sites, including Ar Rasfa in the tributary Wadi az-Zagh.

Northwestern Jordan should have been an attractive area for hominin occupation. Even today, under arid conditions northwest Jordan has the highest rainfall (between 400-800 mm/year) of the country (Bender 1974). It contains abundant relict Mediterranean woodlands, one of the richest sources of plants and animal food in western Eurasia (Zohary 1962). Northwest Jordan was colder during the Late Pleistocene, as evidenced by pollen cores sampled from Jordan Valley (Horowitz 1987), but it was much less cold than higher elevations in southern Jordan at the same time (much as it remains today). The Middle Paleolithic record of northwest Jordan could be every bit as rich as that known from adjacent parts of Israel and the West Bank,

such as Mount Carmel and the Galilee. Similarly, it would be surprising if the Northwest Jordanian Middle Paleolithic evidence was exactly the same as is known either from southern Jordan or the Carmel/Galilee. In either case, the only way to test these hypotheses is by locating sites, excavating them, and describing their contents.

This book provides a detailed description of the lithic assemblage from Ar Rasfa, a Middle Paleolithic site in the Ajlun District (northwestern Jordan). Chapter 2 provides geographic, stratigraphic and contextual information about the Ar Rasfa site. Chapter 3 presents a technological and typological framework for the analysis of stone tools and a preliminary description of the major categories of stone artifacts (i.e., cores, flakes, retouched tools). Chapter 4 presents an analysis of variability among these major artifact categories. The main goal of this analysis is to reconstruct behavioral sources of lithic industrial variability at Ar Rasfa. Chapter 5, the conclusion, compares the lithic evidence from Ar Rasfa to other Middle Paleolithic assemblages from Jordan, the Levant, and Southwest Asia.

CHAPTER 2.

THE AR RASFA SITE AND ITS SETTING

Ar Rasfa is a Middle Paleolithic site in the Ajlun District (northwestern Jordan) in the Jordan Rift Valley. Ar Rasfa is situated in the Jordan valley, north of Wadi az-Zagh, approximately one kilometer north of the lowest point in the Wadi al Yabis (32°24'26.37" N, 35°35'55.01"E at -37 meters below sea level)(Figure 2.1-2.3). The site is a southwest-facing limestone headland above deposits of the Lisan Formation. The name, Ar Rasfa ("Hill of Paving Stones") was provided by local informants, and is apparently derived from a small village north and up-slope from the site. The site is reached from the main Jordan Valley (Ghawr) highway by driving east around to the main hospital in the town of Masharia, along an agricultural road, and then walking to the site about 0.5 km. Local shepherds say that the site can be reached by trackways from Ar Rasfa town as well.

Ar Rasfa lies near the interface of the Lisan Formation's diatomaceous and aragonite facies, suggesting the site was near the southern end of the less-brackish part of the lake that filled the Bashan Basin. Excavation in 1997 and 1999 revealed stratified Levantine Mousterian stone tools in sand and silt deposits overlying gravels. Materials amenable to radiometric dating were not recovered by excavation, and thus the lithic assemblage provides the only information about the antiquity of the site and the "cultural" affinities of the toolmakers.

Figure 2.1 Ar Rasfa region aerial image (modified from Google Earth).

Figure 2.2 Ar Rasfa as seen from above and west, looking east (modified from Google Earth).

Figure 2.3 Ar Rasfa view from northeast (J. Shea Photo).

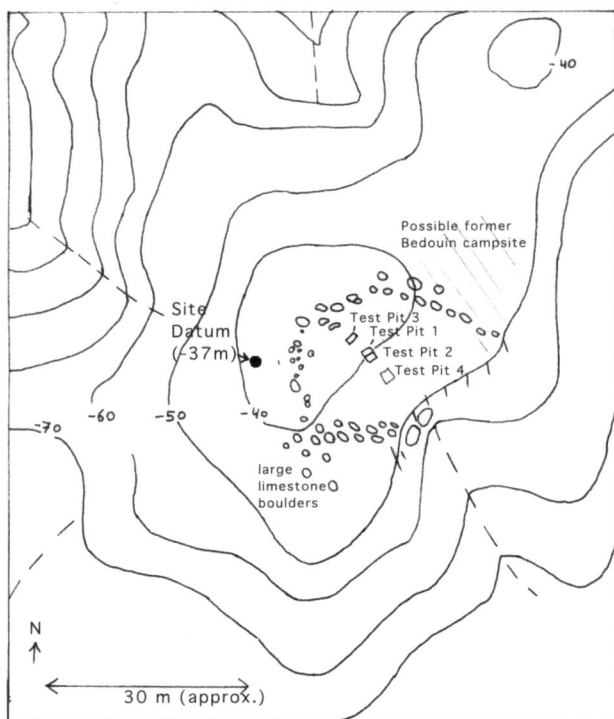

Figure 2.4 Topographic map of site (redrawn after J. Shea notebook sketch).

The Ar Rasfa site itself is on the southeast-facing headland of a limestone promontory jutting southwestward into a small basin formed by the lower Wadi az-Zagh. Middle Paleolithic artifacts occur on the surface of a shallow depression bounded by limestone boulders approximately

100 meters (N-S) by 60 (E-W). Limestone bedrock outcrops at the southwest end of the promontory and forms a steep cliff on the site's western edge. (The site was found during surface survey because stone tools were lying at the bottom of this cliff.) Limestone also outcrops on the eastern edge of the site. There is sparse *Artemisia* and *Zizyphus* vegetation on the site surface. The only visible evidence of post-Paleolithic human activity on the site is the cement foundation of a geodetic marker (now vandalized), several pieces of angle-iron (evidently tent-pegs), and a boulder with both Arabic and English inscriptions carved in it. The latter evidence probably resulted from recent military activity (the site has a commanding view of the Jordan Valley as far as the Israeli town of Beit She'an).

Excavation of Ar Rasfa, 1997-1999

There were two seasons of fieldwork at Ar Rasfa, 1997 and 1999. In 1997, Patricia Crawford discovered the site while she and John Shea were investigating another site downslope (WY101) that had been identified by earlier researchers (Palumbo, et al. 1990). Surface collections were made and four 1 x 1 meter test pits were excavated. The four test pits were aligned approximately northwest-southeast. Test Pits 1 and 2 were contiguous. Test pit 3 was located about 2 meters to the northwest of Test Pit 1. Test Pit 4 was located about two meters southeast of Test Pit 2 (Figures 2.4). In 1999, Shea and Crawford returned to the site and completed the excavation of the deepest of these, Tests Pit 4. Their work at Ar Rasfa was assisted by Mr. Yacoub Maryoud Oweis of the Department of Antiquities Office in Ajlun (Figure 2.5). Excavation initially began using trowels, but shifted to using rock-hammers, as sediment hardness

Figure 2.5 John Shea & Yacoub Oweis excavating at Ar Rasfa in 1997 (J. Shea Photo).

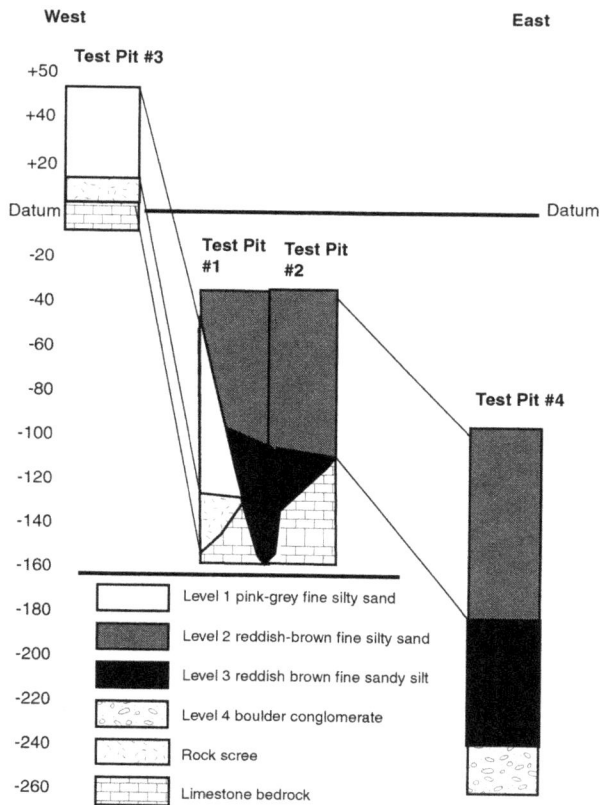

Figure 2.6 Stratigraphy of all test pits.

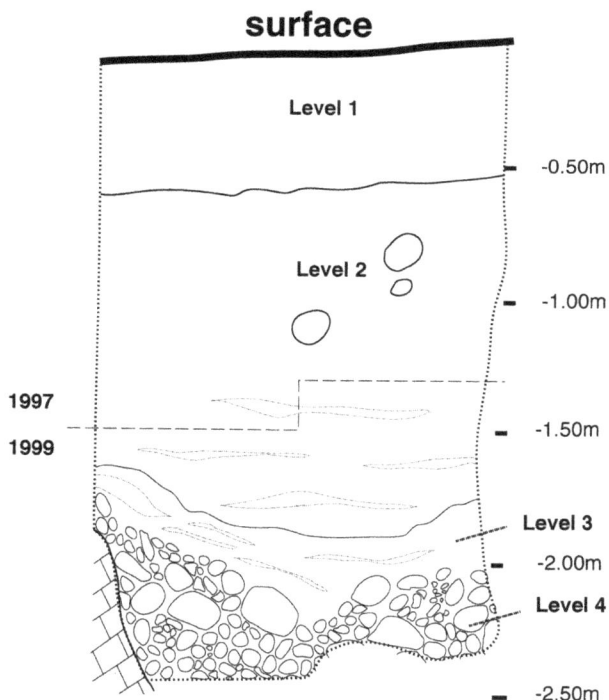

Figure 2.7 Stratigraphy of Test Pit #4.

increased. Excavation proceeded by 10 cm arbitrary levels, stopping at perceived major changes in sediment matrix. All excavated sediment was screened through a 6 mm wire mesh. All lithic artifacts longer than 30mm in any dimension were cataloged individually. Smaller artifacts were bagged together as debris. No faunal remains were recovered. Field laboratory analysis took place on the roof of the Ajlun Castle Hotel. Surface collections were deposited for storage in Ajlun Castle. Excavated finds were deposited at the Department of Antiquities office in Amman.

Shea and Crawford (1999a, 2003) published preliminary reports on Ar Rasfa, based mainly on measurements made on the 1997 excavation collections. No final report was published integrating the more detailed series of technological and typological measurements compiled in 1999. This book presents such a detailed and integrated analysis using the original data records for the Shea-Crawford investigation.

Stratigraphy

The stratigraphy of the Ar Rasfa site probed by Test Pits #1-4 consists of six major units (see Figure 2.6).

Level 1 is a fine silty sand, pinkish-grey in color (Munsell 7.5 YR 6/2) with some rolled and sub-angular limestone fragments (Figures 2.7-2.8). This level was encountered mainly in Test Pit #1 and the western part of Test Pit#2. In both trenches it sits directly on top of rock scree. Stone tools in this layer exhibited moderate patination and edge-damage, suggesting possible disturbance in antiquity.

Level 2 is between 100-110cm thick, a reddish-brown (Munsell 5YR 4/3) fine silty sand with isolated large sub-angular limestone cobbles (10-15 cm in diameter). This level formed the uppermost stratum of Test Pits 1, 2, and 3. Stone tools in Level 2 exhibited minimal patination and/edge-damage, but they quickly turned a whitish color on exposure to direct sunlight. Many artifacts also had carbonate concretions on them. The lower 50cm of Level 2 featured ashy lenses, white in color (Munsell 7.5YR 8/1) about 2 cm in maximum thickness and between 30-60 cm in horizontal extent.

Level 3 is fine sandy silt, a reddish brown in color (Munsell 5YR 4/4) and between 5-15 cm thick. This level sat directly on top of a either bedrock (in Test Pits 1 and 20 or a boulder conglomerate (Level 4) comprised of rounded flint and subangular limestone boulders between 5-15cm in diameter (Figure 2.9). The majority of lithic artifacts from Ar Rasfa were recovered from Levels 2 and 3. No differences in lithic artifact preservation were noted between tools excavated from these levels.

Level 4 is, as noted above, a conglomerate. The matrix holding its cobbles and boulders together was identical to Layer 3. Many flint artifacts were found on top of this boulder layer, and this is the reason it was designated an archaeological level. These artifacts were patinated white,

Figure 2.8 Ar Rasfa Test Pit #4 North Baulk stratigraphy (J. Shea photo).

Figure 2.9 Ar Rasfa Test Pit #4 North Baulk contact between Levels 3 and 4 (conglomerate)(J. Shea photo).

Figure 2.10 Artifacts from Ar Rasfa Test Pit #4, contact between Levels 3 and 4 (J. Shea Photo).

but otherwise showed little evidence of edge damage other than that incurred during excavation (Figure 2.10).

Tables 2.1-2.3 summarize the occurrence of artifacts by different excavation units of the four test pits. Test Pits 1, 2, and 4 show a similar pattern. In most levels, flakes and flake fragments outnumber cores. All three of these test pits show the same pattern of artifact frequency with increased depth. Artifact densities are initially low, they increase gradually, peaking between 50-150cm below datum, and declining beyond that point. This final decline at the bottom of the test pits reflects the exposure of bedrock or sterile conglomerate. Artifacts were found on the surface of the conglomerate, but not within it.

Shea's preliminary investigations failed to demonstrate significant technological or typological differences either along stratigraphic lines or between test pits. Therefore, this study treats the totality of the Ar Rasfa collection as a single assemblage.

Analytical Procedures

All artifacts larger than 2.5 cm were given an individual catalog number (AR97 or AR99, depending on the year of the excavation) and an unique artifact identification number. The artifact registry/catalog also recorded the test pit number and the stratigraphic level from which each artifact was recovered.

The analytical variables recorded for cores and flakes/

retouched flakes differed from one another, and they are described separately below, together with justifications for their use. All measurements were made using digital scales (to the nearest whole gram) or digital calipers (to the nearest whole millimeter).

Cores

In this analysis, cores were defined as lithic artifacts featuring at least one complete conchoidal fracture scar greater than 30mm from initiation to termination.

A. CORE ATTRIBUTES

Core Type refers to one of a series of general core categories taken from standard typologies for Lower and Middle Paleolithic assemblages in Africa, Europe, and the Near East (Bar-Yosef and Goren-Inbar 1993, Bordes 1961, Debénath and Dibble 1994, Goren-Inbar 1990, Hovers 2009, Leakey 1971). These core types included the following:

1. Battered Cobble/Hammerstone/Tested Piece –clast (pebble/cobble) or angular rock fragment featuring small fractures, pitting and crushing damage indicating repeated use as a percussor against hard materials.
2. Chopper –pebble core with a working edge around less than 2/3 of the circumference.
3. Discoid –pebble core with a working edge around the circumference.

4. Polyhedron –angular rock fragment with multiple working edges.
5. Levallois core –flat core with one extensively-worked flake-release surface and a second less-extensively-worked striking platform surface.
6. Prismatic core/Core-scraper –hemispherical pebble core with a worked edge around its circumference.
7. Core-on-Flake –flake showing evidence of striking platform preparation (on a truncation) and an adjacent flake-release surface.
8. Other –described in comments.
9. Core fragment

It is possible there are behavioral and/or functional differences among these types, but the principal justification for their use here is to enable straightforward comparisons with other Paleolithic assemblages.

Scar Directionality refers to the alignment of scars on the most-extensively-worked surface of the core (Boëda et al. 1990, Geneste 1985). The following general categories were used to characterize this variable:

1. Unidirectional-Parallel –scars are approximately parallel to each other.
2. Unidirectional-Convergent –scars converge at the distal end of the surface.
3. Radial/Centripetal –scars converge at the center of the flake-release surface.
4. Bidirectional-Opposed –scars converge towards one another's distal ends.

In principle at least, a competent knapper can use any one of these methods to detach a flake of any chosen size or shape with equal effectiveness. Nevertheless, it is also likely that scars with opposed or intersecting trajectories (i.e., radial/centripetal and bidirectional-opposed) will likely predominate among flakes detached after prolonged core-reduction, as decreased core size brings striking platform surfaces closer together.

Shape of Largest Complete Scar –the overall plan view shape of the largest flake scar on the most-extensively-worked surface of the core.

1. Point/triangle
2. Blade/rectangle
3. Flake/square, oval, or irregular

The analytical value of this variable is speculative. It may shed light on patterned variation in knapping strategies that may be correlated with core reduction. If, for example, blades/rectangular flakes (which preserve high ratios of circumference relative to area) were being detached as part of a strategy to conserve core mass, one might expect blade scars to predominate among smaller cores.

Cortex Extent refers to the amount of the core surface that preserves weathered external surface, or cortex. No distinction was drawn between cortex reflecting the former surface of a nodule and cortical surfaces formed by abrasion. Following Andrefsky's (2005) recommendation that the three categories of cortex extent yield the most reliable and replicable observations, this attribute was characterized as follows:

0. None
1. 1-33%
2. 34-66%
3. 67-100%

Cortex extent decreases during the initial stages of core reduction. Thus, this variable is a relative measure for the point in core reduction when a particular flake was detached. Though there are circumstances in which cortical flakes can persist to near the end of a core reduction sequence (e.g., one in which cortical surfaces were preferred for lateral edges or striking platform surfaces). Nevertheless, replicative knapping experiments suggest that flakes with extensive cortical surfaces result from earlier stages of core reduction while those wholly free of cortex predominate in later stages of core reduction.

B. Core Measurements

Most of the measurements made on cores are standard practices in the analysis of Lower and Middle Paleolithic assemblages. Most are simply various measures of overall artifact size and call for no special comment.

Mass in grams was measured with an Acculab™ analytical balance.

Maximum Length in mm was measured between the two most distant points on the core (i.e., the core's long axis).

Maximum Width in mm was measured between the two most distant points on the core perpendicular to long axis of the core.

Maximum Thickness in mm was measured between the two most distant points on the core in the dimension perpendicular to the plane defined by the cores length and width.

Length in mm of Last Scar was measured for the last-removed scar on the most extensively-worked surface of the core. This was measured in order to discriminate Levallois from non-Levallois cores.

Length of Worked Edge in mm was measured along the worked edge.

Circumference in mm was measured along the same plane as the worked edge. This was measured in order to express the relative extent of the worked edge on the core in a way independent of actual core size. Cores that have been reduced superficially will exhibit similar low values for the ratio between worked edge and circumference, whereas those that have been extensively exploited will exhibit values close to parity or greater (≥ 1.0).

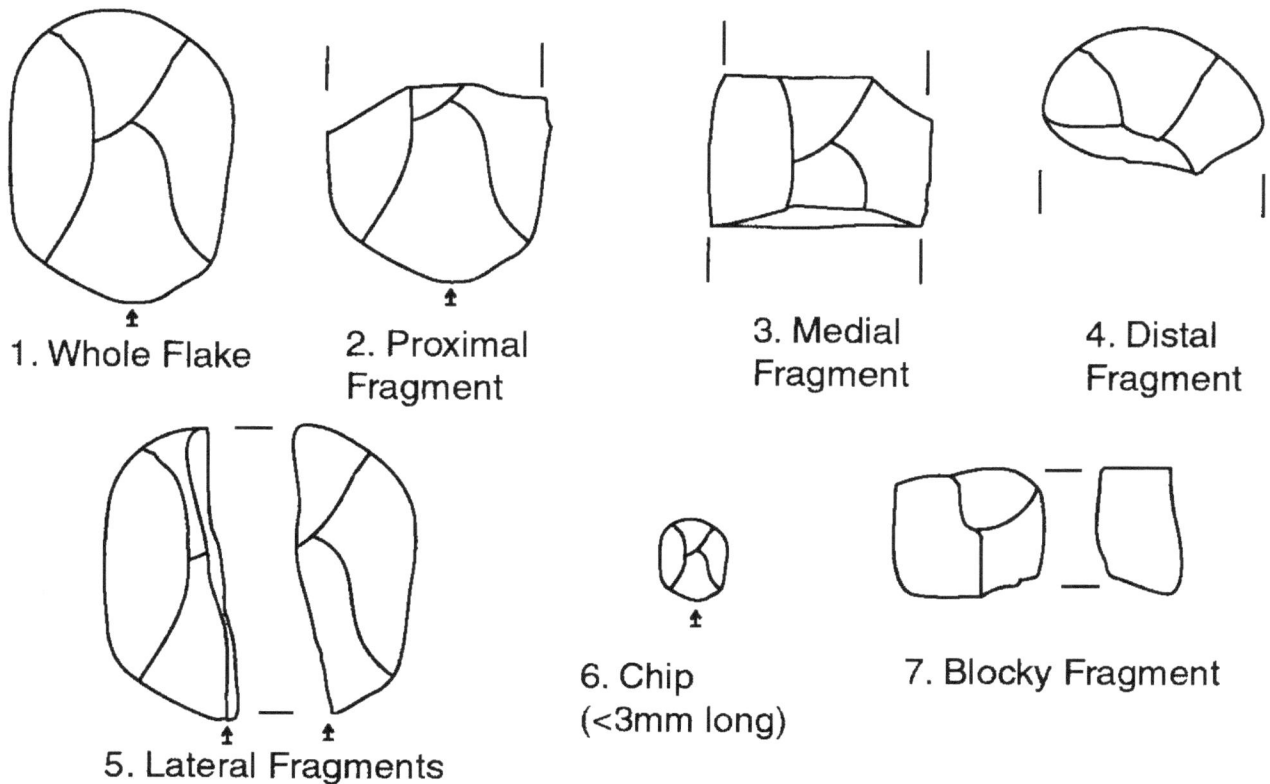

Figure 2.11 Flake completeness.

Count of Scars >30mm in length was a simple tally of the number of flake scars on all core surfaces longer than 30 mm from inception to termination. In principle, the number of such flake scars ought to increase with greater core reduction, though in practice the relationship is curvilinear –because smaller cores, by virtue of their size, present fewer opportunities for flakes to propagate more than 30mm.

(The size cutoff of 30mm for flake scar counts and for debitage measurement [see below] is an arbitrary one, and reflects archaeological convention. Archaeologists' use of this convention has to be treated skeptically. There are many ethnographic examples of humans using stone tool shorter than 30mm. Microwear analyses of from nearly all phases of Stone Age prehistory report use-related wear on artifacts less than 30mm long.)

Débitage (Flakes & Flake Fragments [>30 mm long])

Flakes and flake fragments are fracture products detached from cores larger than 30mm from initiation to termination. In describing these artifacts, this analysis follows the standard convention of referring to the striking platform and point of percussion as the "proximal" and the point of fracture termination as the "distal". That surface of the flake comprising the former exterior surface of the core is the "dorsal" and the newly-fractured surface on the opposite side of the flake from the dorsal is termed the "ventral" face.

A. Débitage Attributes

Technological Tool Type refers to a series of broadly-defined artifact-types adapted from traditional Middle Paleolithic typology (for detailed descriptions of these types, see Debénath and Dibble 1994).

1. Levallois Point
2. Levallois Blade
3. Levallois Flake
4. Core-Trimming Flake
5. Naturally Backed Blade
6. Whole (unretouched) Flake
7. Retouched Tool
8. Flake Fragment
9. Blocky Fragment
10. Other

As with core-types, these artifacts are recognized by archaeological convention/tradition (Debénath and Dibble 1994) rather than by any knowledge about their functional stylistic significance grounded in middle-range research.

Completeness describes whether or not the flake preserves striking platform, distal termination, and lateral edges. It is classified in the following terms (see Figure 2.11):

1. Whole Flake
2. Proximal Flake Fragment
3. Medial Flake Fragment
4. Distal Flake Fragment
5. Lateral Flake Fragment
6. Chip or Debris (<30mm long)
7. Blocky Fragment
8. Other

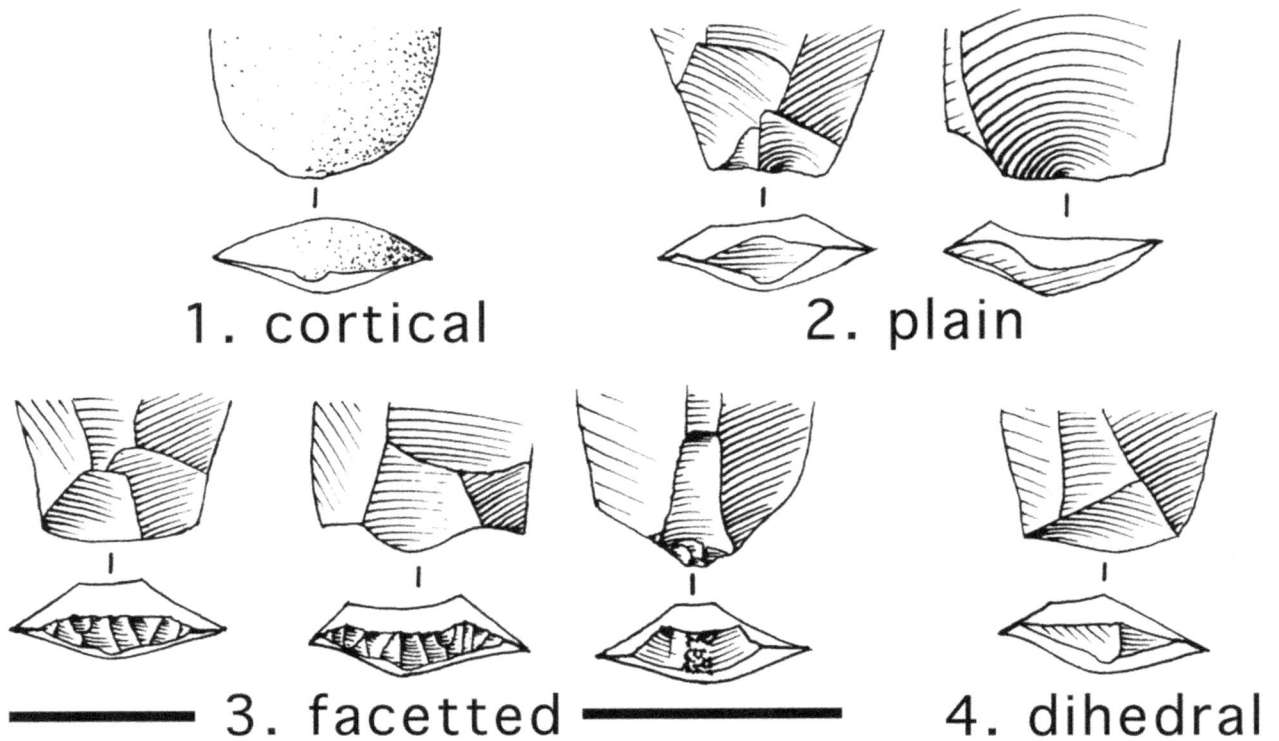

Figure 2.12 Flake striking platform morphology (Modified after Inizan et al. (1999)).

These categories of flake completeness are not often used as stand-alone descriptions of Lower and Middle Paleolithic tools (Debénath and Dibble 1994). Rather, they are customarily employed as subsets of major morphological tool types. Here, they are used as a second, independent method for characterizing débitage variation, one more in line with standard practices in North American prehistoric archaeology (Andrefsky 2005, Sullivan and Rozen 1985).

Striking Platform Morphology was classified according to a simple taxonomy modified after Inizan *et al.* (1999) (see Figure 2.12).

0. Absent;
1. Cortical
2. Plain
3. Facetted
4. Dihedral
5. Other

These categories of striking platform morphology are thought to reflect a continuum of greater or lesser core reduction. Cortical and plain platforms are thought to predominate in early stages of core reduction, while facetted and dihedral ones are though to reflect later stages. There is experimental support for these interpretations, though, the relationship is complex. For example, many knappers construct facetted or dihedral platforms in the initial stages of core reduction in order to precisely control flake removals.

Distal-Proximal Symmetry refers to the location of maximum thickness in distal-proximal plane of the flake (see Figure 2.13).

1. Proximal
2. Medial
3. Distal
4. Even

The most effective flake release surfaces on cores are mildly excurvated (outwardly curving). As successive "generations" of flakes are removed along the same axis, they typically terminate ever shorter (i.e., closer to the point of fracture initiation). The process creates a distal convexity that, at some point, has to be undercut by a deeply-propagating flake in order for the flake release surface to remain productive. In principle, this variable helps one to identify flakes struck in the service of flake-release-surface maintenance (those with "distal") values from those struck in the routine course of core exploitation.

Medio-Lateral Symmetry refers to the location of maximum thickness in the medio-lateral plane of the flake (see Figure 2.14).

1. Right
2. Center
3. Left
4. Even

The analytical value of this variable is similar to distal-proximal symmetry. Flakes whose thickness values are skewed either right or left can be seen as the results of

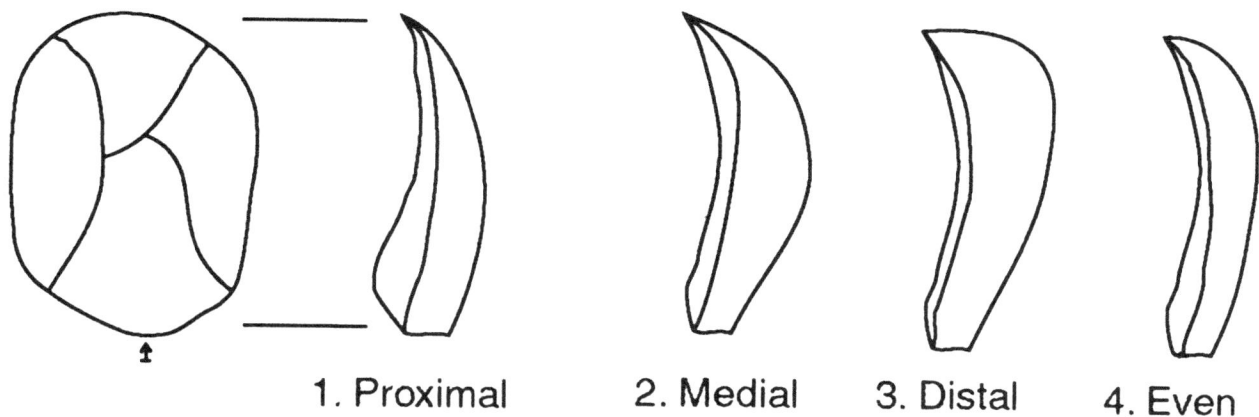

Figure 2.13 Flake distal-proximal symmetry.

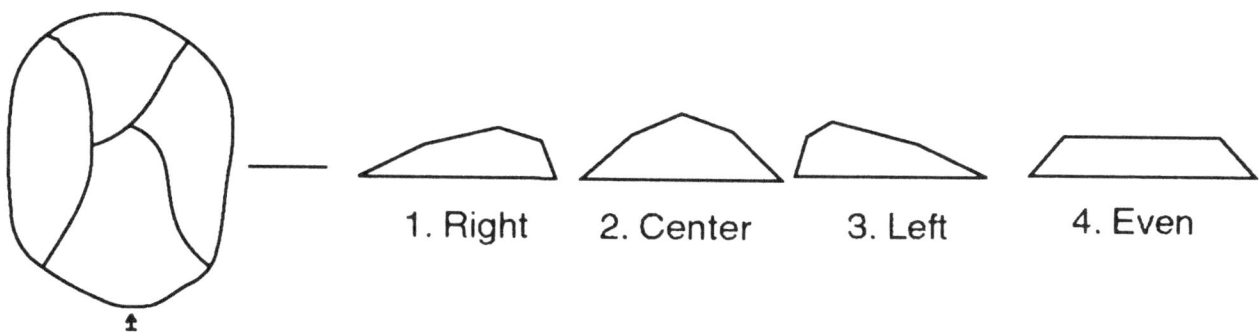

Figure 2.14 Flake medio-lateral symmetry.

efforts to remove convexities from the lateral margins of flake release surfaces. However, and unlike flakes with thick distal ends (whose "gain" in thickness risks lateral snapping), a strong case can be made (Sandgathe 2004) that flakes with one steep, easily-grasped, edge may have been desirable débitage products in their own right.

Dorsal Surface Morphology refers to a classification of the surface in comparison to a series of templates (see Figure 2.15).

1. All Cortical
2. Partially Cortical -Distal
3. Partially Cortical -Right
4. Partially Cortical -Left
5. Relict Edge -Distal
6. Relict Edge -Right
7. Relict Edge -Left
8. Unidirectional-Parallel Flake Scars
9. Unidirectional-Convergent Flake Scars
10. Radial/Centripetal Flake Scars
11. Bidirectional-Opposed Flake Scars
12. Other
13. Indeterminate

These templates incorporate some of the classifications of scar directionality discussed previously, but as a group they appear here for the first time (as near as we can determine). Their use reflects a more nuanced classification of "core-

trimming elements" (flakes with relict edges on their non-proximal margins), as well as of cortical flakes. The use of these flake dorsal surface morphology classifications here is, in a sense, an "investment", because similar classificatory frameworks are known to be in use for descriptions of Levantine and other Middle Paleolithic assemblages now in preparation for publication.

B. Débitage Measurements

Figure 2.16 shows the following measurement taken on flakes. As with cores, those measurements of maximum dimensions measure raw size and call for no special comment. The technological measurement and measurements of striking platform dimensions are used to calculate several technological ratios, most notably width/thickness, flake surface area/thickness and striking platform width/striking platform thickness that are used for comparative purposes.

Maximum Length in mm was measured between the two most distant points on the flake.

Technological Length in mm was measured from the point of impact to point opposite on distal end.

Maximum Width in mm was measured between the two most distant points of right and left lateral edges.

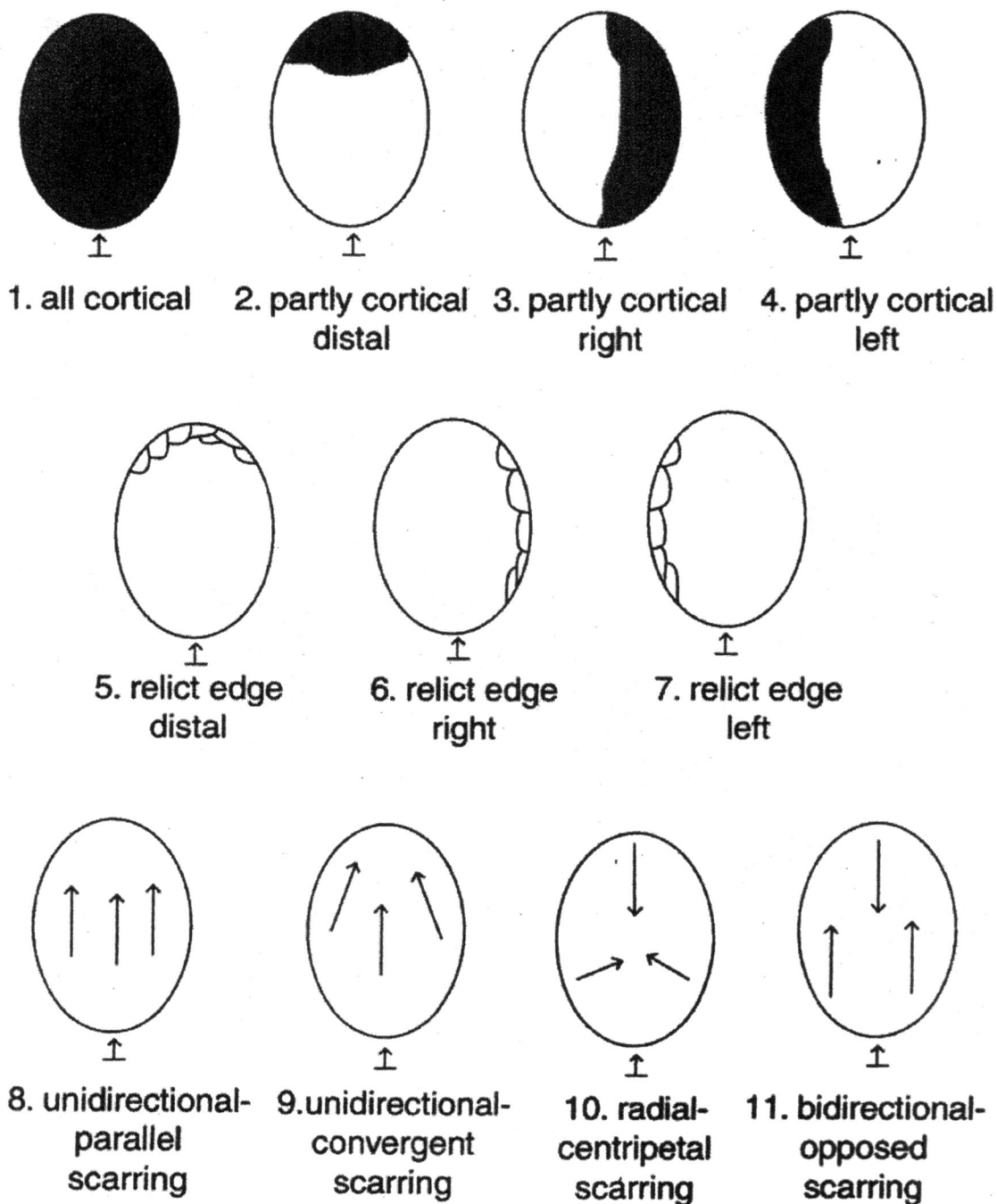

Figure 2.15 Flake dorsal surface morphology.

Maximum Thickness in mm was measured between the two most distant points on the dorsal and ventral surfaces perpendicular to the plane defined by the technological length and width axes.

Striking Platform Width in mm was measured between the two most distant points on the striking platform along the plane defined by the intersection of dorsal and ventral surfaces.

Striking Platform Thickness in mm was measured between point of impact and the closest point at which striking platform surface and dorsal surface intersect with one another.

Midpoint Width in mm is flake width measured at midpoint of length and perpendicular to the technological long axis.

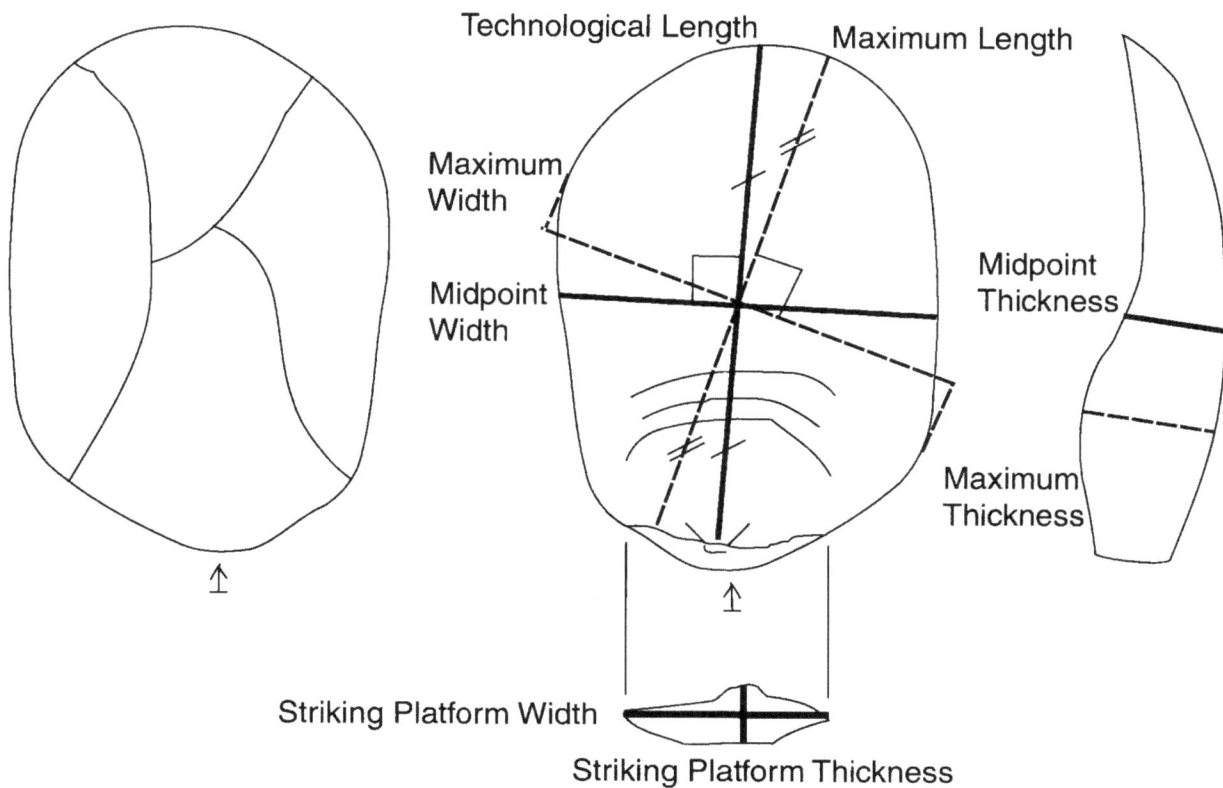

Figure 2.16 Flake measurements.

Midpoint Thickness in mm is the thickness of the flake measured at the intersection of technological length and width axes.

Cortex Extent expressed the extent of weathered cortical surface on the dorsal side of the flake.

  0. None
  1. 1-33%
  2. 34-66%
  3. 67-100%

As with cores, in principle this variable measures the degree of core surface modification prior to flake detachment.

Retouched Tools

Retouched tools are flakes and flake fragments that have continuous and patterned clusters of flake scars along at least a portion of their circumference. Retouch may be unifacial (flakes removed from one side alone), bifacial (flakes removed both faces of the same edge), or alternating (flakes removed from dorsal and ventral faces of different edges)(Inizan et al. 1999). Retouch is usually differentiated from incidental edge damage and use-related microfracturing by being continuous and invasive for more than 3 mm from initiation to termination along an edge. Burination is considered a kind of retouch, even though it is possible that the burin flakes were desired blanks for tools.

In principle, cores that have been shaped by retouch (e.g., handaxes) are considered retouched tools, but they should be more properly classified as objects simultaneously satisfying the criteria for cores and retouched tools.

A. RETOUCHED TOOL ATTRIBUTES

All of the same attribute characterizations made for flakes and flake fragments were also made for individual retouched tools. These attributes included the following (for descriptions see above): completeness, striking platform morphology, cortex extent, distal-proximal symmetry, medio-lateral symmetry, and dorsal surface morphology.

Morphological Retouched Tool Type: Individual retouched tools were classified in terms of a simplified morphological typology, as follows:

  1. Transverse scraper –flake with a retouched distal end.
  2. Sidescraper –flake with one or more retouched lateral edges.
  3. Backed Knife –elongated piece with one steeply-retouched lateral edge and another unretouched edge opposite.
  4. Notch –artifact with one or more retouched concavities.
  5. Denticulate –artifact with jagged, irregular retouch along at least one edge.

6. Awl –artifact with a short, thick retouched point defined by concave edges.
7. Burin –artifact with a burin removal scar
8. Truncated-Facetted Piece –flake with a truncation on one or more edges
9. Combination Tool –retouched tool combining more than one of the retouch types above (e.g., double sidescraper, transverse and side scraper, notch and denticulate, etc.).
10. Other (see comments).

As with core and debitage morphological types, these categories reflect traditional archaeological descriptive conventions (Debénath and Dibble 1994). This analysis does not further subdivide these major artifact categories into specific Bordian artifact-types. There being no evidence that the 62 named artifact-types in Bordes (1961) typology represent either stylistically or functionally-distinct taxa, the effort of classification cannot be justified in terms of its likely analytical value.

Location of Retouched Edge: For each retouched tool a note was made about whether or not retouch was present on the distal end, the proximal end, the right lateral edge, and/or the left lateral edge. Further measurements were made on each of these individual retouched edges (see below).

B. RETOUCHED TOOL MEASUREMENTS

The following measurements were made on retouched tools in more or less the same way as for unretouched flakes and flake fragments (for descriptions, see above): **Maximum Length, Technological Length, Maximum Width, Maximum Thickness, Striking Platform Width, Striking Platform Thickness, Midpoint Width, Midpoint Thickness**. The justification for these measurements is similar. They serve as measures of overall size, and, inversely, of the amount of potential tool utility remaining in them at the point when/where they were discarded.

Retouched Edges

Traditional Paleolithic stone tool typology tends to treat stone tools as unitary wholes, that is, they treat all of the edges on a tool as if they were functionally related to one another and used at the same time. Numerous ethnographic studies of stone tool use, particularly stone tool use by mobile human groups (Gould et al. 1971, Hayden 1979, White 1968), suggest this may be an erroneous assumption. For many stone tool users, individual edges are the focus of attention, rather than the whole tool. In other words, the "tool" is merely an aggregation of potential and actual functional edges. (It bears remembering that the tool types used to describe archaeological assemblages were created by archaeologists with little actual experience making or using stone tools.) Taking into account the possibility that prehistoric humans thought about stone tools in similar ways to ethnographic stone-tool-users, we recorded a series of measurements that allow retouched edges to be analyzed independently of the tools on which they are located. The nearest analogy to this would be a comparative study of

modern-day utility knives that compared variation in the configuration of individual blades (knives, scissors, corkscrews, pliers) as well as variation at the level of whole tools (e.g., Swiss Army Knives™ vs. Leatherman™ tools).

A. RETOUCHED EDGE ATTRIBUTES

The principal attributes recorded for retouched edges were their position on the tool, retouch mode, and their shape in plan view.

Position of Retouched Edge on the tool was recorded in terms of quadrants (distal, proximal, right lateral, left lateral) and in terms of whether or not retouch was present. This variable allows a simple method for quantifying the extent of retouch on a tool independently of actual artifact size.

Retouch Mode was classified as follows:

1. Dorsal face only
2. Ventral face only
3. Bifacial and continuous
4. Burin
5. Alternating

The use of this variable reflects traditional archaeological descriptive conventions (Debénath and Dibble 1994). Whether or not these different modes of retouch retain significant functional or stylistic significance remains unknown.

Shape in Plan View was classified as follows:

1. Point
2. Convex
3. Straight
4. Concave
5. Recurved
6. Denticulate

These classifications of edge shape in plan view vary along with reduction, albeit in complex ways (Dibble 1995). Retouched edge shape in plan view is also a key variable in traditional Middle Paleolithic systematics, and recording it here, in theory at least allows interested and motivated researchers to place these artifacts within traditional typological frameworks.

B. RETOUCHED EDGE MEASUREMENTS

The continuous measurements made on retouched edges included invasiveness and spine-plane angle.

Invasiveness was measured in terms of the length in whole millimeters of the most invasive flake scar on a retouched edge. In principle, the more times an edge is retouched, the further across the flaked edge a flake has to travel in order to re-establish an acute functional edge. Thus, invasiveness or retouch is generally seen as reflecting greater degrees of edge modification, if not resharpening (Eren et al. 2005, Kuhn 1990).

Spine-Plane Angle was measured indirectly, by using a simple trigonometric formula to calculate the angle from edge thickness measured at a point 5 mm in from the retouched edge (Dibble and Bernard 1980). The resulting angle was calculated to the nearest whole degree. Edges with thicker spine plane angles require greater energy in order to penetrate a worked material. In principle, therefore, steeper edges reflect more-heavily retouched tools. Any such inference, however, has to be weighed against the possibility that edges of differing acuteness may have been selected for differing cutting tasks (i.e., steeper edges for orthogonal cutting [scraping] or for use against hard materials)(Semenov 1964, Wilmsen 1968).

CHAPTER 3.

DESCRIPTION OF LITHIC ARTIFACTS

This chapter describes the lithic assemblage from the Ar Rasfa site. In turn, it discusses cores, débitage (flakes and flake fragments), and retouched tools. For each of these technological artifact categories variation in discrete variables is discussed first, then variation in continuous variables.

Cores

Table 3.1 tabulates the cores from Ar Rasfa in terms of major technological and typological categories. Figures 3.1-3.8 show a selection of cores from Ar Rasfa. These include Levallois cores (Figures 3.1-3.5), choppers (Figure 3.6), and cores-on-flakes (Figures 3.7-3.8).

The majority of cores from Ar Rasfa are Levallois cores. Choppers (11.1%) and cores-on-flakes are the two next-most-common core-types. That the second and third most common core types are relatively expedient (i.e., cores minimally modified from their original form) suggests Ar Rasfa was a primary tool making site, a place where tools were knapped in close proximity to raw material sources.

Table 3.1 Core types.

Core Type	n	%
Battered Cobble	3	1.0
Chopper	32	11.1
Core Fragment	3	1.0
Cores-on-Flakes	27	9.3
Discoid	19	6.6
Levallois Core	158	54.7
Other	20	6.9
Polyhedron	5	1.7
Prismatic Core	22	7.6
Total	289	100.0

a. Core Attributes

Forty-nine percent of cores preserve between 1-33% cortex. These, plus cores with 34-66% cortex, amount to 80% of the cores from Ar Rasfa (see Table 3.2). A relatively high proportion of cores with cortex on them suggest the site is located near the primary source of raw materials (Odell 2004: 27).

Table 3.2 Cores: Variation in cortex coverage.

Core Type	None		1-33%		34-66%		>67%		Total	
	n	%	n	%	n	%	n	%	n	%
Battered Cobble		0		0		0	3	12	3	1
Chopper		0	8	6	12	13	12	48	32	11
Discoid	3	9	13	9	2	2	1	4	19	7
Polyhedron	1	3	3	2	1	1		0	5	2
Levallois Core	14	41	83	59	54	61	7	28	158	55
Prismatic Core		0	15	11	6	7	1	4	22	8
Cores-on-Flakes	11	32	11	8	5	6		0	27	9
Core Fragment	1	3	1	1	1	1		0	3	1
Other	4	12	7	5	8	9	1	4	20	7
Total	34	100	141	100	89	100	25	100	289	100
%	12		49		31		9		100	

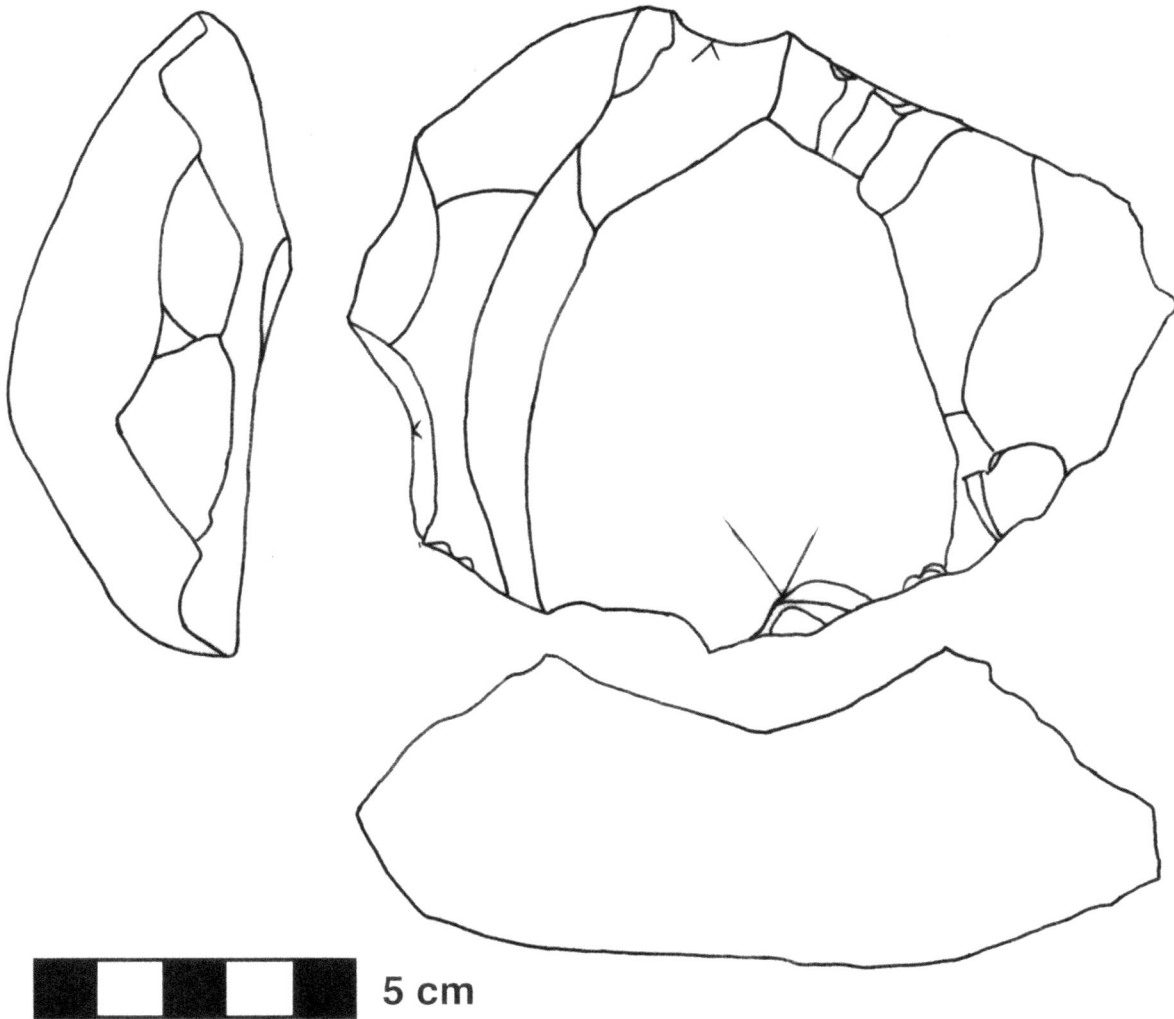

5 cm

Figure 3.1. Cores: Large Levallois core, bidirectional-opposed preparation (WY97.14.74).

Table 3.3 Cores: Variation in scar directionality.

Core Type	UniPll		UniCvg		RadCnt		BiOp		Other		Total	
	n	%	n	%	n	%	n	%	n	%	n	%
Battered Cobble	1	3		0		0		0	2	4	3	1
Chopper	8	26	3	8	2	4	1	1	2	4	16	7
Discoid		0	1	3	3	6		0		0	4	2
Polyhedron		0		0	1	2	1	1		0	2	1
Levallois Core	19	61	32	80	45	85	60	88	2	4	158	66
Prismatic Core		0	3	8		0	3	4		0	6	3
Cores-on-Flakes	1	3		0		0	3	4	23	49	27	11
Core Fragment		0		0	1	2		0	2	4	3	1
Other	2	6	1	3	1	2		0	16	34	20	8
Total	31	100	40	100	53	100	68	100	47	100	239	100
%	13		17		22		28		20		100	

Abbreviations:
UniPll = Unidirectional Parallel
UniCvg= Unidirectional-Convergent
RadCnt = Radial-Centripetal
BiOp = Bidirectional-Opposed

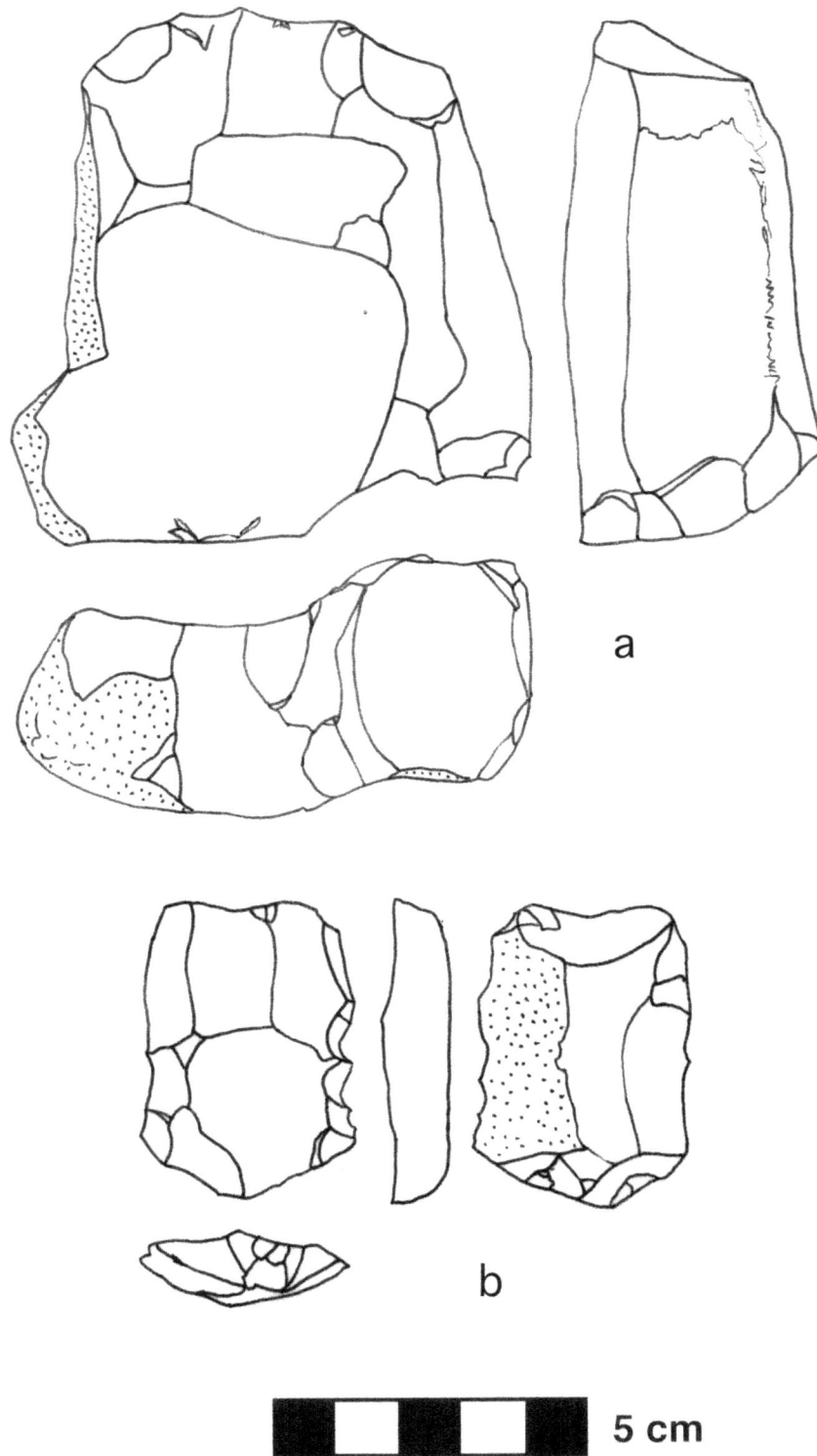

Figure 3.2. Cores: a. Levallois core with bidirectional-opposed preparation (AR97.351), b. small Levallois core with bidirectional-opposed preparation (ID number illegible).

The most common pattern of scar directionality on cores is bidirectional-opposed (28 %). This and radial/centripetal scar directionality total 50% of the cores from Ar Rasfa (see Table 3.3). Bidirectional-opposed and radial/centripetal scar directionality are common consequences of intense core reduction (Kuhn 1995). Their prominence in the Ar Rasfa

assemblage may further indicate "in bulk" flake production at the site.

The shape of the largest complete scar on 64 % of cores is that of a "flake" (i.e., a square, oval, or irregular shape). Cores with a "pointed" or triangular-shaped largest

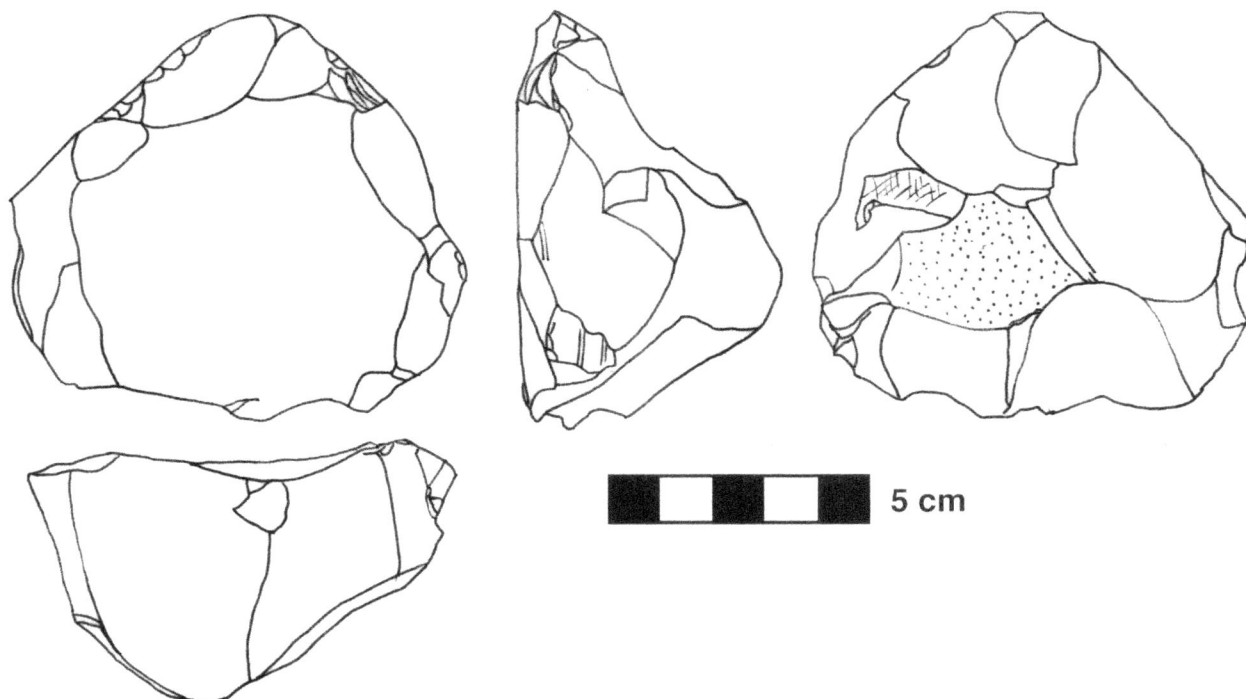

Figure 3.3. Cores: Levallois core with radial/centripetal preparation (WY.AR.1E.379).

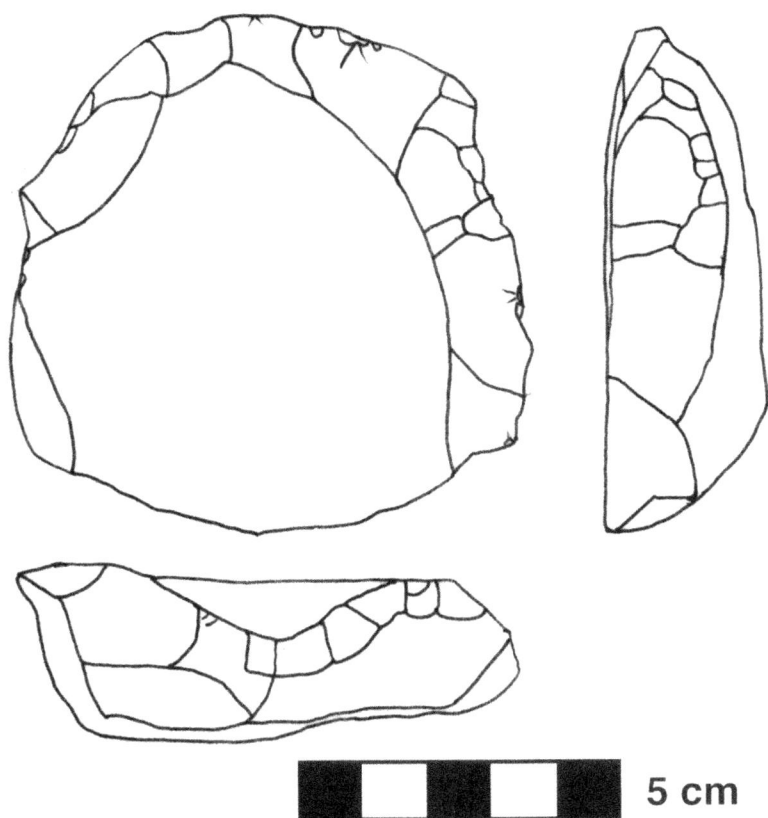

Figure 3.4. Cores: Levallois core with radial/centripetal preparation (WY97. AR.1W.1).

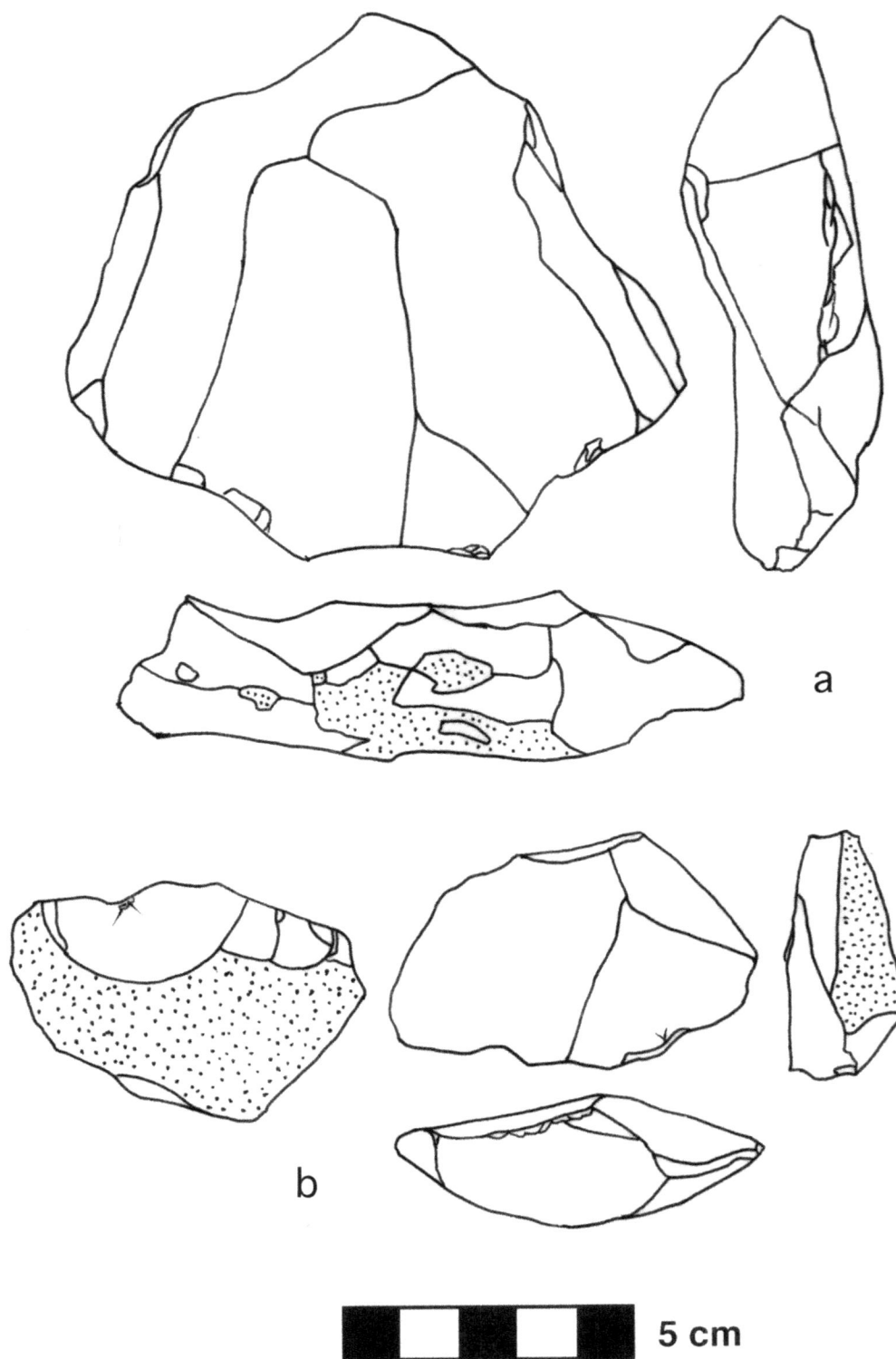

Figure 3.5. Cores: a. Levallois core with unidirectional-convergent preparation (WY97.AR.1E.376), b. Small Levallois core with unidirectional-convergent preparation (WY97.AR.1E.402).

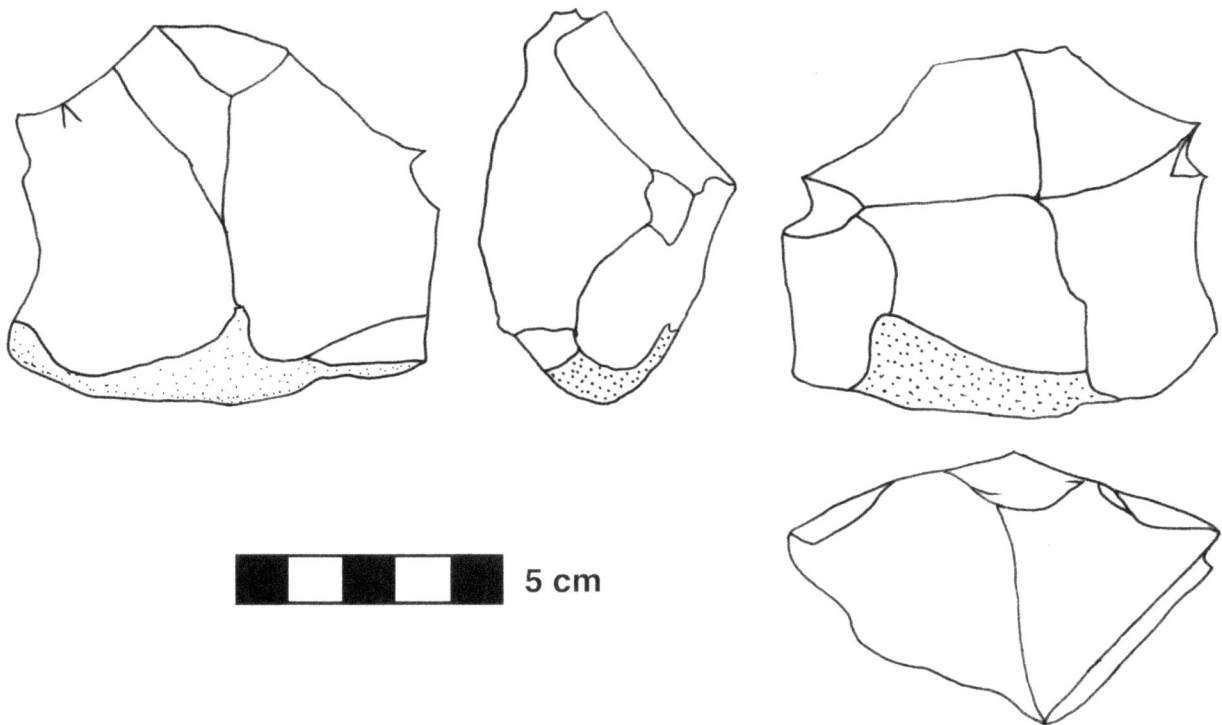

Figure 3.6. Cores: Chopper (AR99.450).

Figure 3.7. Cores: Core-on-flake (AR99.238).

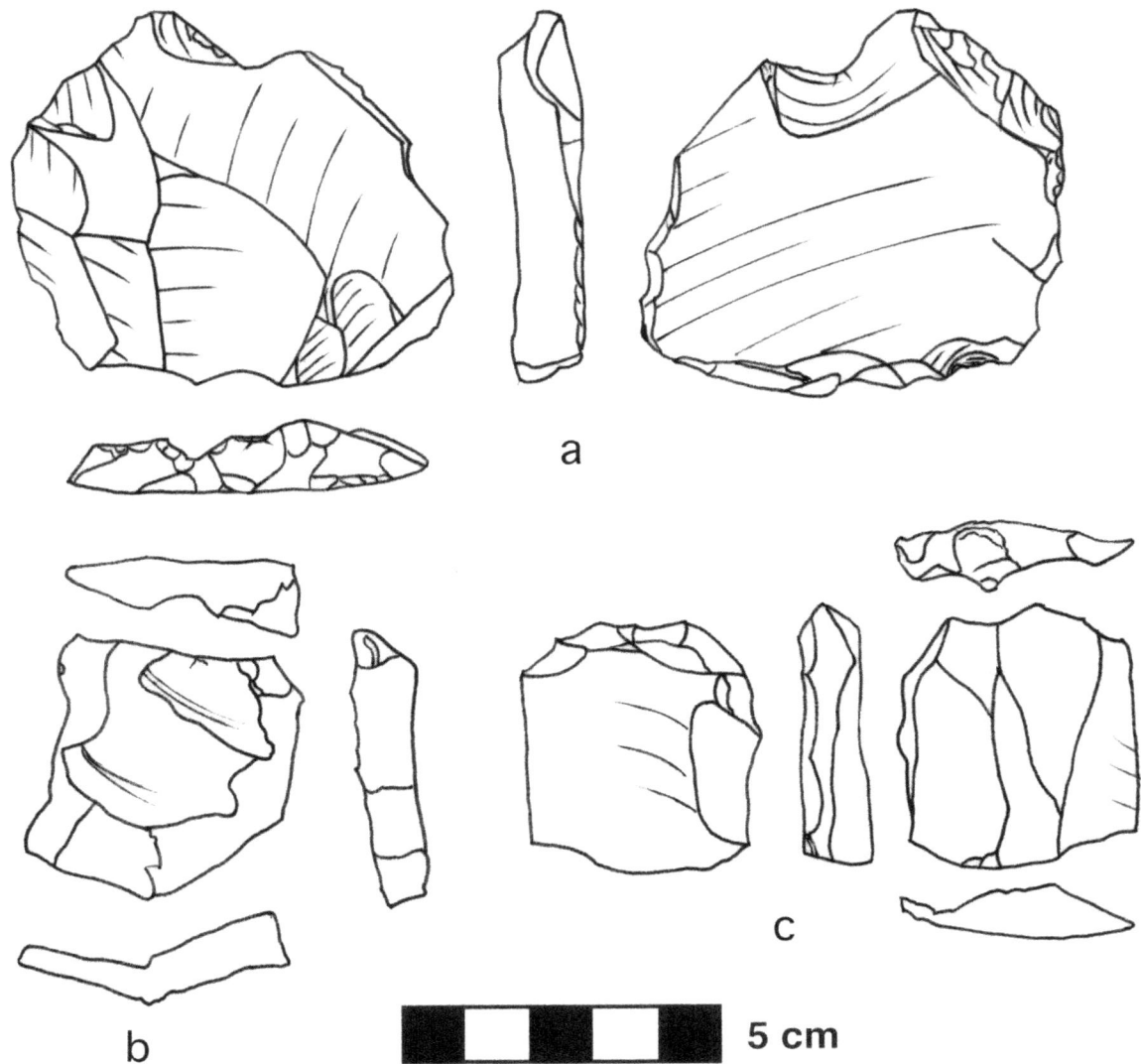

Figure 3.8. Cores: Cores-on-flakes (a. WY97.AR.TP4.4, b. AR99.61, c. AR99.63).

complete scar amount to 23% of cores from Ar Rasfa (see Table 3.4). This is a common pattern among Levantine Mousterian assemblages (Kaufman 1999, Meignen and Bar-Yosef 1988, Munday 1979, Shea 2003b).

b. Core Measurements

Choppers have the highest average mass among the core types (119 g). The second highest average mass is for Levallois cores (92 g), then discoids (73 g). Most cores exhibit wide variation in mass except polyhedrons, which are consistently small (see Table 3.5). This pattern of declining core mass, from choppers to discoids and polyhedrons, is similar to ones noted in many Paleolithic assemblages, from Plio-Pleistocene times onwards (Potts 1988). Levallois cores show mass values intermediate between choppers and discoids, and discoids are heavier than polyhedrons. This could suggest that choppers, Levallois cores, discoids and polyhedrons are components of a single core-reduction sequence that were abandoned at different stages of reduction. The only evidence potentially contradicting this hypothesis is the wide variation in mass values for choppers. Such variation could reflect some choppers being small cobbles that were exploited casually for flakes and not reduced further. Alternatively, the different cores may be functionally different tools whose uses are in some way correlated with their different mass values.

In terms of length, choppers and Levallois cores are the longest cores on average. The relative length of choppers probably reflects minimal modification from original cobble size. The length of Levallois cores almost certainly reflects knappers' efforts to maintain long (or generally extensive) flake-release surfaces, thereby to maximize the size and/or potential utility of the flakes detached from them (Chazan 1997, Davis 2000, Sandgathe 2004). Except for core fragments, all cores show considerable variation in maximum length (see Table 3.6).

Table 3.4 Cores: Shape of largest complete scar.

Core Type	Point		Blade		Flake		Indet.		Total	
	n	%	n	%	n	%	n	%	n	%
Battered Cobble		0		0	3	2		0	3	1
Chopper	3	5	2	5	27	15		0	32	11
Discoid	2	3	2	5	15	8		0	19	7
Polyhedron	1	2		0	4	2		0	5	2
Levallois Core	41	63	25	66	90	49	2	100	158	55
Prismatic Core	7	11	6	16	9	5		0	22	8
Cores-on-Flakes	9	14	2	5	16	9		0	27	9
Core Fragment	1	2		0	1	1		0	2	1
Other	1	2	1	3	18	10		0	20	7
Total	65	100	38	100	183	100	2	100	288	100
%	23		13		64		1		100	

Table 3.5 Cores: Descriptive statistics for mass (g).

Core Type	Mean	SD	Max.	Min.	n
Battered Cobble					
Chopper	119	88	351	27	11
Discoid	73	54	221	17	15
Polyhedron	51	24	76	29	3
Levallois Core	92	65	422	18	115
Prismatic Core	67	40	133	16	13
Cores-on-Flakes	47	26	124	13	20
Core Fragment					
Other	54	43	175	24	12
Total	82	62	422	13	189

Table 3.6 Cores: Descriptive Statistics for maximum length (mm).

Core Type	Mean	SD	Max.	Min.	n
Battered Cobble	55	13.2	65	40	3
Chopper	65.3	12.7	92	42	32
Discoid	55.4	14.5	87	36	19
Polyhedron	57.4	22.1	94	34	5
Levallois Core	62.8	15.6	150	20	158
Prismatic Core	57	15.2	93	35	22
Cores-on-Flakes	58.2	11.5	78	36	27
Core Fragment	54	1.7	56	53	3
Other	64	18.2	114	34	20
Total	61.5	15.2	150	20	289

Table 3.7 Cores: Descriptive statistics for maximum width (mm).

Core Type	Mean	SD	Max.	Min.	n
Battered Cobble	38.3	11.2	51	30	3
Chopper	53.7	12.3	82	32	32
Discoid	46.3	13.2	80	25	19
Polyhedron	40.8	13.7	60	27	5
Levallois Core	52.1	15.4	150	25	158
Prismatic Core	44.9	12.1	68	22	22
Cores-on-Flakes	44.4	9.9	66	30	27
Core Fragment	34	14	48	20	3
Other	43.9	15.6	88	25	20
Total	49.6	14.6	150	20	289

Table 3.8 Cores: Descriptive statistics for maximum thickness (mm).

Core Type	Mean	SD	Max.	Min.	n
Battered Cobble	27.7	4	30	23	3
Chopper	33.9	6.9	50	21	32
Discoid	26	9	51	16	19
Polyhedron	29.6	6.7	36	21	5
Levallois Core	26.5	11.5	100	1	158
Prismatic Core	28.3	9.5	45	16	22
Cores-on-Flakes	17.7	5.6	32	9	27
Core Fragment	18.7	6.4	26	15	3
Other	25.2	11.3	66	13	20
Total	26.5	10.8	100	1	289

Table 3.9 Cores: Descriptive statistics for length of last scar (mm).

Core Type	Mean	SD	Max.	Min.	n
Battered Cobble	21.7	12	34	10	3
Chopper	35.7	11.1	63	13	27
Discoid	27.2	8	42	11	19
Polyhedron	30	6.6	35	19	5
Levallois Core	40.4	17	140	6	156
Prismatic Core	35.9	11.6	59	15	19
Cores-on-Flakes	34.2	10.1	65	20	27
Core Fragment	43	na	43	43	1
Other	36.1	14.9	65	14	16
Total	37.4	15.2	140	6	273

Choppers are the widest among core types on average (see Table 3.7). Next widest are Levallois cores, then discoids. Standard deviation values for maximum width of entire cores are about equal, except cores-on-flakes which are relatively small. That the mean width values for minimally-modified choppers differ by only a few millimeters from those of extensively-modified Levallois cores could reflect efforts by the Ar Rasfa knappers to maintain cores capable of producing broad flakes with relatively high potential for curation by resharpening.

Choppers are the thickest core type on average. Most other core types exhibit similar values (between 25-30 mm) except cores-on-flakes, which are much thinner than other cores (average 17.7 mm). In terms of standard deviation, discoids, Levallois cores and prismatic cores are more variable than other core types (see Table 3.8). The greater variability in thickness associated with Levallois cores and prismatic cores may reflect the availability of raw material sources nearby. Absent selective pressure to maximize flake yields caused by raw material scarcity, one would expect to see wide variability in the dimensions of the more heavily modified core types.

The longest mean values for length of last scar are for Levallois cores (40.4 mm) and prismatic cores (35.9 mm), both of which share a stable hierarchy of flake-release and striking platform surfaces. For each, this hierarchy enables knappers to maximize the length of flakes detached from the flake-release surface. Levallois cores exhibit greatest variation in this variable (see Table 3.9).

The highest average value for length of worked edge is for discoids (143.2). This is followed by the values for polyhedrons (139.0 mm) and Levallois cores (100.8 mm). The likely cause of this somewhat counterintuitive finding is that average values for discoids and polyhedrons are skewed by a small number of large specimens. The greatest variation in length of worked edge is found with discoids, polyhedrons and Levallois cores (see Table 3.10)

Circumference is highest on average among choppers (193.4 mm). The next highest value is for Levallois cores (186.7 mm), but most core circumference values fall within a narrow range of values (140-174 mm). On average, prismatic cores and polyhedrons show the greatest variability (see Table 3.11). Most of these differences are auto-correlates with mass and other variables related to overall size.

Levallois cores on average have the highest number of flake scars greater than 30 mm long (6.4). However, their values are only barely higher than those for polyhedrons (6.2) and discoids (6.2 mm). There are relatively few differences in the variability of this length of the largest flake scar among the various core types (see Table 3.12).

Débitage: Flakes and Flake Fragments

Figures 3.9-3.15 show drawings of flakes from Ar Rasfa, including Levallois products (Figure 3.9-3.12) and core-trimming elements (Figures 3.13-3.14). Table 3.13 lists total numbers of different kinds of flakes and flake fragments

Table 3.10 Cores: Descriptive statistics for worked edge (mm).

Core Type	Mean	SD	Max.	Min.	n
Battered Cobble	14	14.4	30	2	3
Chopper	67.9	41.9	160	7	32
Discoid	143.2	55.9	255	20	19
Polyhedron	139	91.1	255	45	5
Levallois Core	100.8	50.2	245	10	158
Prismatic Core	71.4	33.2	170	35	22
Cores-on-Flakes	47.7	31.5	125	10	27
Core Fragment	32.5	31.8	55	10	2
Other	79.5	49.9	170	20	19
Total	90.6	53.4	255	2	287

Table 3.11 Cores: Descriptive statistics for circumference (mm).

Core Type	Mean	SD	Max.	Min.	n
Battered Cobble	140	26.5	170	120	3
Chopper	193.4	43.5	320	100	32
Discoid	165.2	44.2	255	105	19
Polyhedron	177	54.5	255	120	5
Levallois Core	186.7	47.2	500	105	158
Prismatic Core	170.7	53.4	330	90	22
Cores-on-Flakes	166.1	33.2	250	115	27
Core Fragment	162.5	17.7	175	150	2
Other	174.7	53.6	340	100	19
Total	181.2	46.8	500	90	287

Table 3.12 Débitage: Variation in number of flake scars >30 mm long.

Core Type	Mean	SD	Max.	Min.	n
Battered Cobble	1.3	1.5	3	0	3
Chopper	3.6	3.1	12	0	31
Discoid	6.2	3.7	11	0	18
Polyhedron	6.2	3.8	12	2	5
Levallois Core	6.4	3.7	17	0	152
Prismatic Core	3.6	2.9	9	0	21
Cores-on-Flakes	2.5	2.4	7	0	26
Core Fragment	3	1	4	2	3
Other	3.2	2.1	7	0	20
Total	5.2	3.7	17	0	279

Table 3.13 Débitage: Counts of technological flake types.

Technological Type	Total	%
Levallois Point	61	4.3
Levallois Blade	34	2.4
Levallois Flake	179	12.5
Core-Trimming Flake	80	5.6
Naturally-Backed Flake	7	0.5
Whole Flake	670	47.0
Retouched Tool	108	7.6
Non-Proximal Flake Fragment	198	13.9
Proximal Flake Fragment	79	5.5
Blocky Fragment	11	0.8
Total	1427	100.0

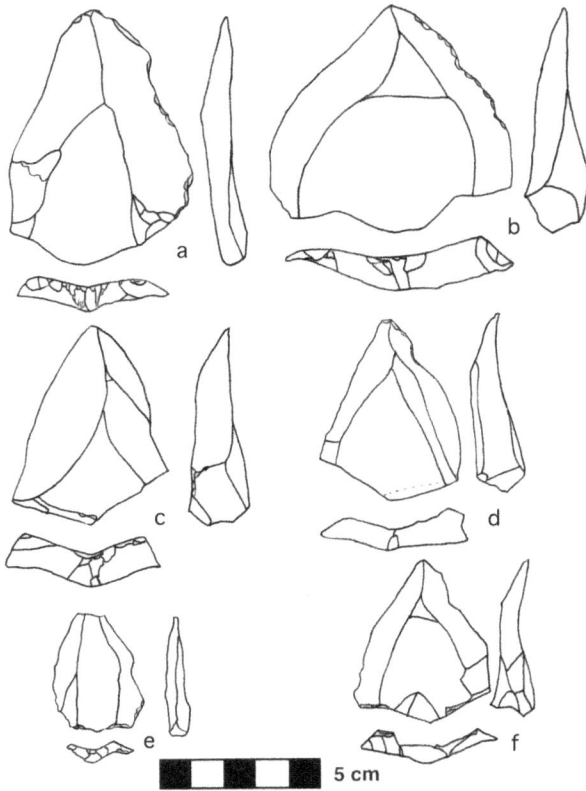

Figure 3.9. Débitage: Levallois points (a. WY97. AR.4.385, b. WY97.AR.2.67, c. WY97.AR.1e.264, d. AR99.406, e. AR99.443, f. WY97.AR.1E.209).

from Ar Rasfa. Whole flakes account for the highest percentage of débitage. Flake fragments and Levallois flakes are the second and third highest percentages of all detached pieces.

a. Débitage Attributes

Table 3.14 shows the cross-tabulation between major tool types and technological categories of completeness. Of the 1427 artifacts, 72% (n = 1031) are entire flakes, 28% (n = 400) are fragments of flakes. Of entire flakes only 27% (n = 289) are Levallois. The remainders are entire non-Levallois flakes (65%), core-trimming flakes (8%) or naturally-backed flakes (1%). Among flake fragments the 108 retouched tools account for 27%. The remainder (50%) is mostly non-proximal flake fragments.

Seventy-eight percent of all débitage has striking platforms. Among these, the majority (74%) has facetted striking platforms. Plain striking platforms (18%) are the next most common striking platform type (see Table 3.15). The predominance of facetted platforms suggests an emphasis on careful core preparation. The scarcity of cortical platforms may indicate that much core reduction took place off-site, or in a part of the site that was not sampled by excavation.

Fifty percent of débitage has no cortex on its dorsal surface. These and tools with 1-33% cortex amount to 74% of débitage from Ar Rasfa (see Table 3.16). This proportion

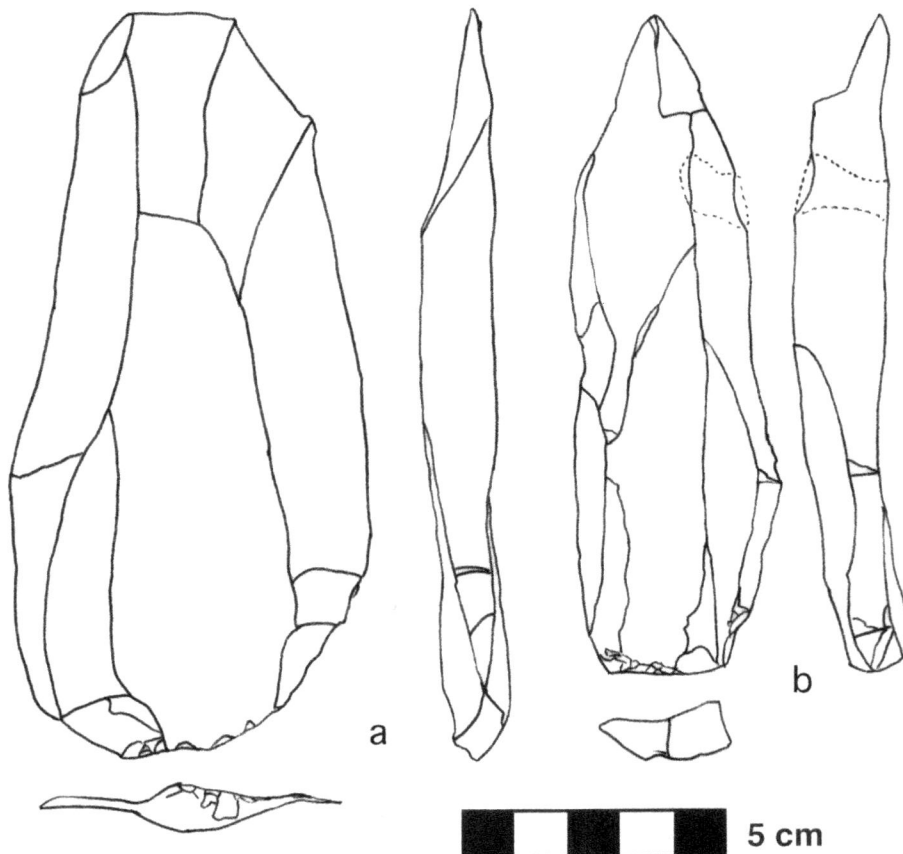

Figure 3.10. Débitage: Levallois flakes, blades (a. AR99.397, b. AR99.158).

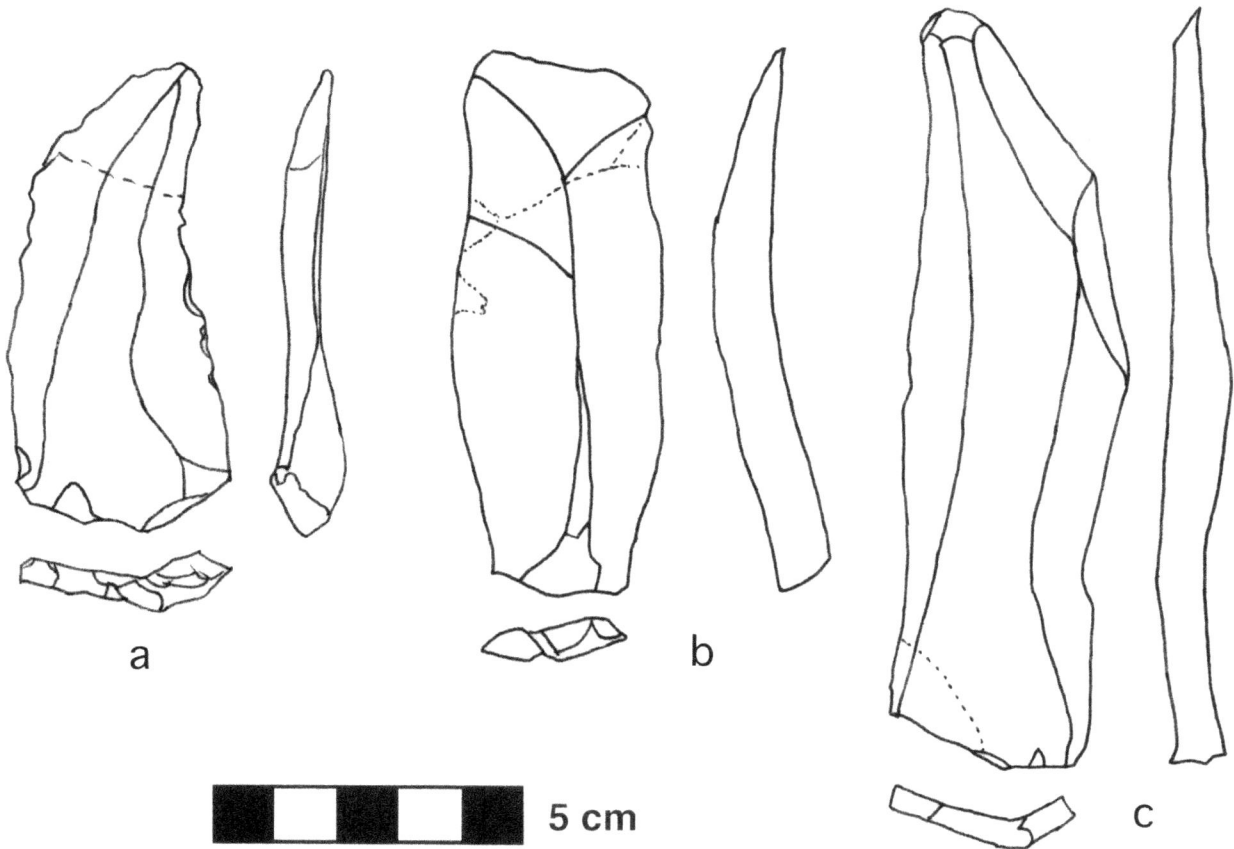

Figure 3.11. Débitage: Levallois flakes (a. AR99.89, b. AR99.459, c. AR97.443).

Table 3.14 Débitage: Technological types vs. completeness.

Technological Type	Whole flake		Proximal flake fragment		Medial flake fragment		Distal flake fragment	
	n	%	n	%	n	%	n	%
Levallois Point	57	6	4	3		0		0
Levallois Blade	34	3		0		0		0
Levallois Flake	172	17	4	3	1	2	1	1
Core-Trimming Flake	71	7	6	5		0	2	1
Naturally-Backed Flake	7	1		0		0		0
Whole Flake	636	62	13	10	3	6	12	7
Retouched Tool	57	6	18	15	14	28	13	8
Non-Proximal Flake Fragment		0		0	32	64	139	82
Proximal Flake Fragment		0	79	64		0		0
Blocky Fragment		0		0		0	2	1
Total	1034	100	124	100	50	100	169	100
%	72		9		4		12	

of cortex-free and minimally-cortical débitage probably reflects prolonged and intensive core reduction on site. If reduction had been short-term and expedient, then one would expect higher proportions of cortical débitage (Parry and Kelly 1987).

In terms of distal-proximal symmetry, 39% of flakes are thickest at their proximal end (see Table 3.17). These and flakes that are thickest in medial aspect amount to 62% of Ar Rasfa débitage. This is the normal pattern for flakes struck from cores with minimal distal core-rejuvenation. This is a particularly common outcome of radial-centripetal core reduction, where distal convexities are maintained by successive lateral flakes (Meignen and Bar-Yosef 1992).

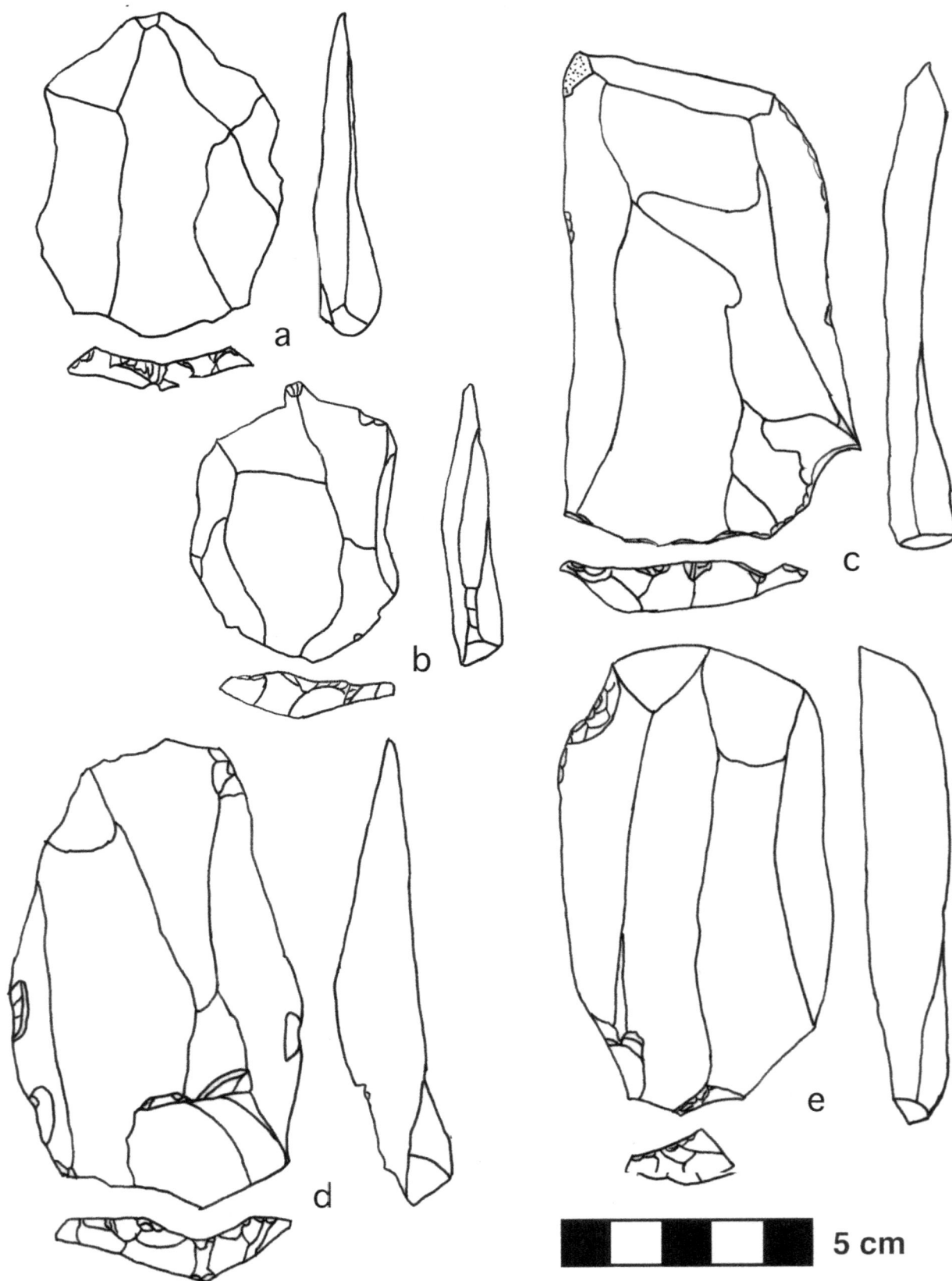

Figure 3.12. Débitage: Levallois flakes (a. AR97.339, b. AR97.345, c. AR97.101, d. AR97.382, e. AR97.109).

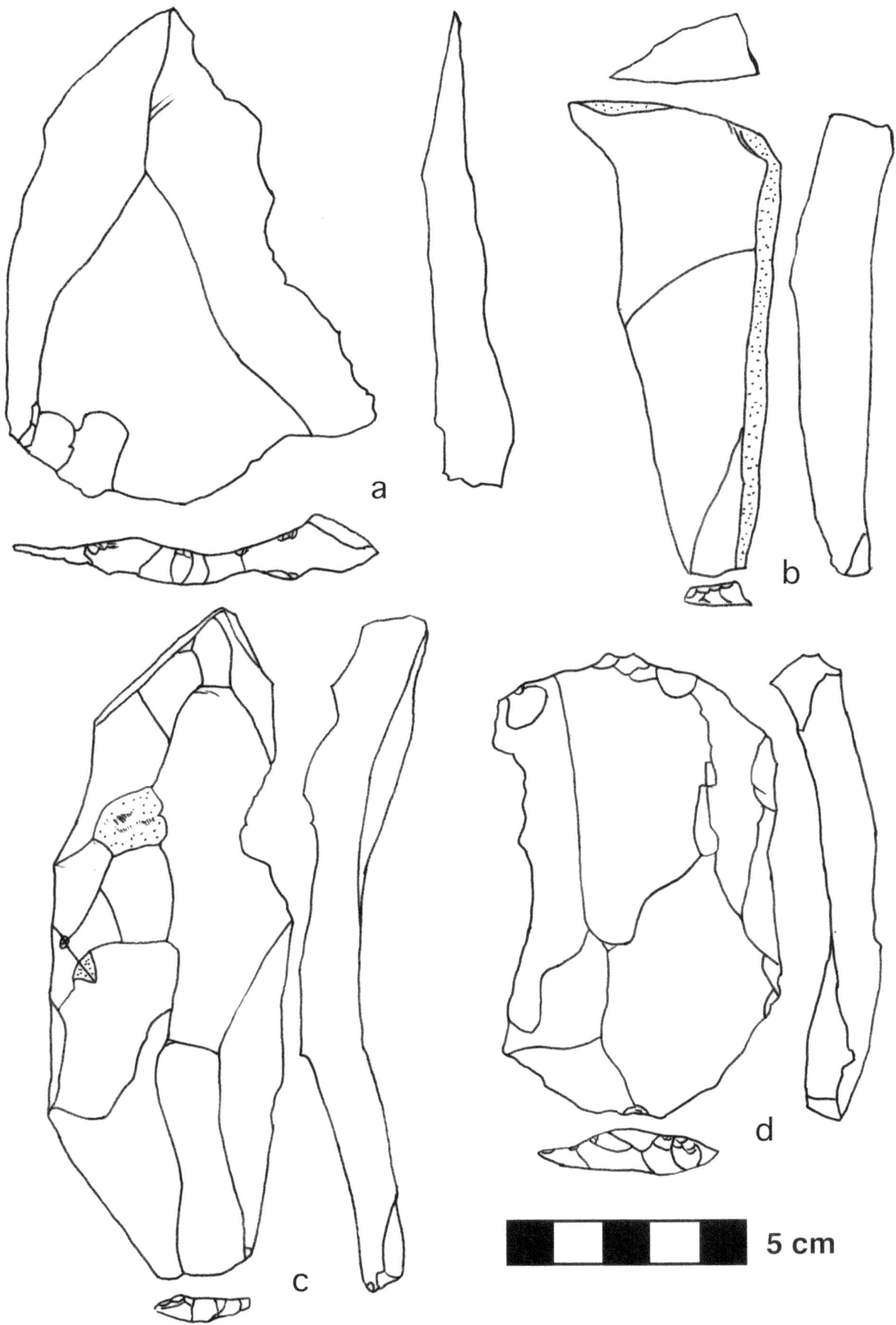

Figure 3.13. Débitage: Core-trimming flakes (overshot flakes/blades)(a. AR97.169, b. AR97.14.83, c. AR97.200, d. AR.97.50).

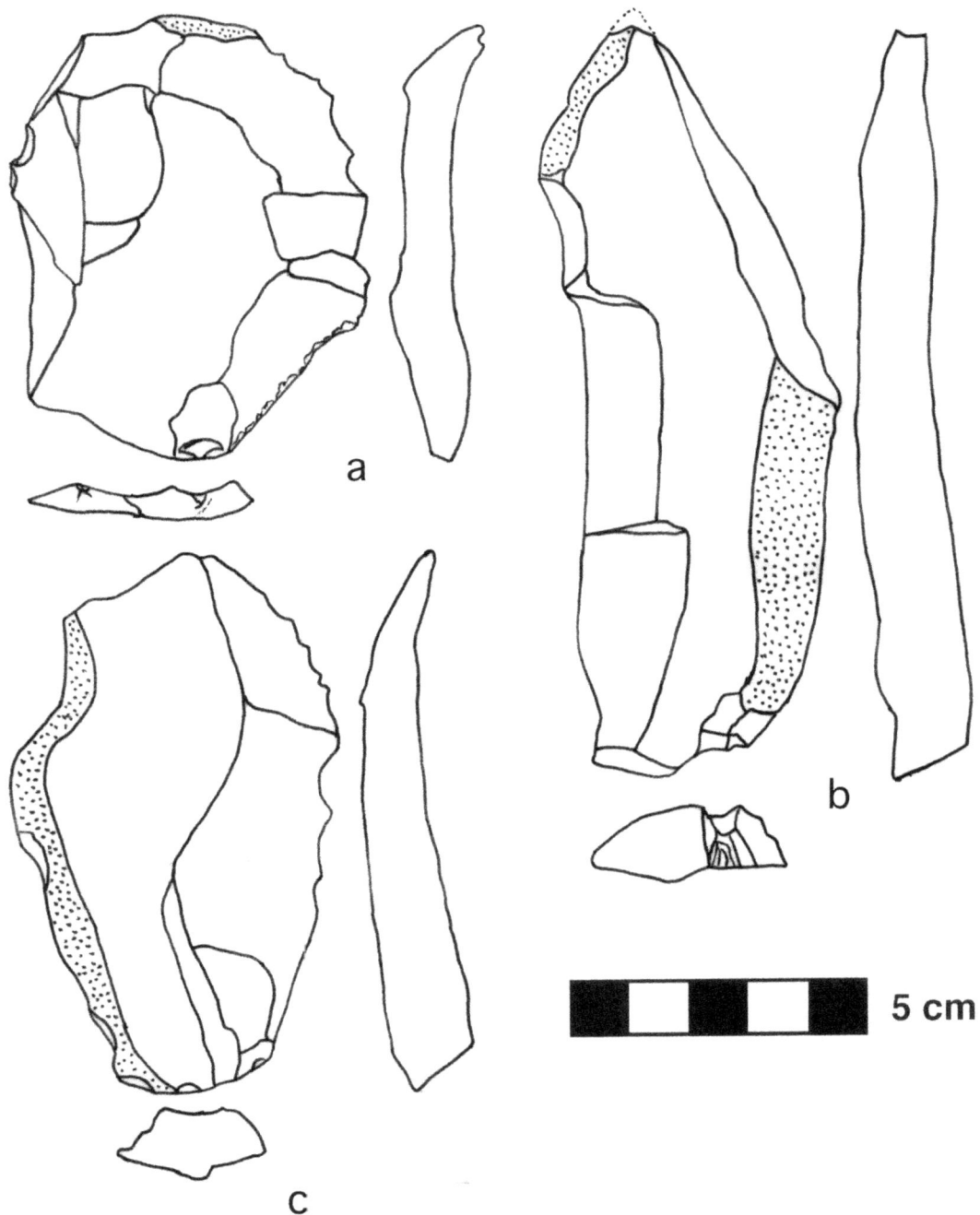

Figure 3.14. Débitage: Cortical core-trimming flakes (a. AR97.214, b. AR97.241, c. AR97.240).

The scarcity of distal thickness values suggests that "overshot" flakes were not common.

In terms of medio-lateral symmetry, 58% of detached pieces are thickest at their center, or "medio-laterally symmetrical" (see Table 3.18). The second highest percentage is to the left of the medio-lateral plane. Together, flakes thickest at their center and to the left medio-laterally total 76 % of débitage. This pattern could reflect either a bias towards clockwise core rotation and/or efforts to preserve the functionality of the part of the tool where distal and right lateral edges converge.

There are three major categories of dorsal surface morphology among the Ar Rasfa débitage: cortical surfaces, surfaces with relict edges, and surfaces with patterned flakes scars (see Table 3.19). Cortical surfaces are the most common (47%), and these are about evenly distributed among the major attribute-states (all cortical, partly cortical distal/right/left). Flakes with relict edges on their dorsal surface amount to only 4% of all the débitage. These relict edges are about evenly distributed on the distal, right-lateral and left-lateral edges. Among flakes with multiple scars on them, the most common patterns are unidirectional-parallel (13%) and bidirectional-convergent (12%). Unidirectional-convergent-preparation is the least-commonly-represented

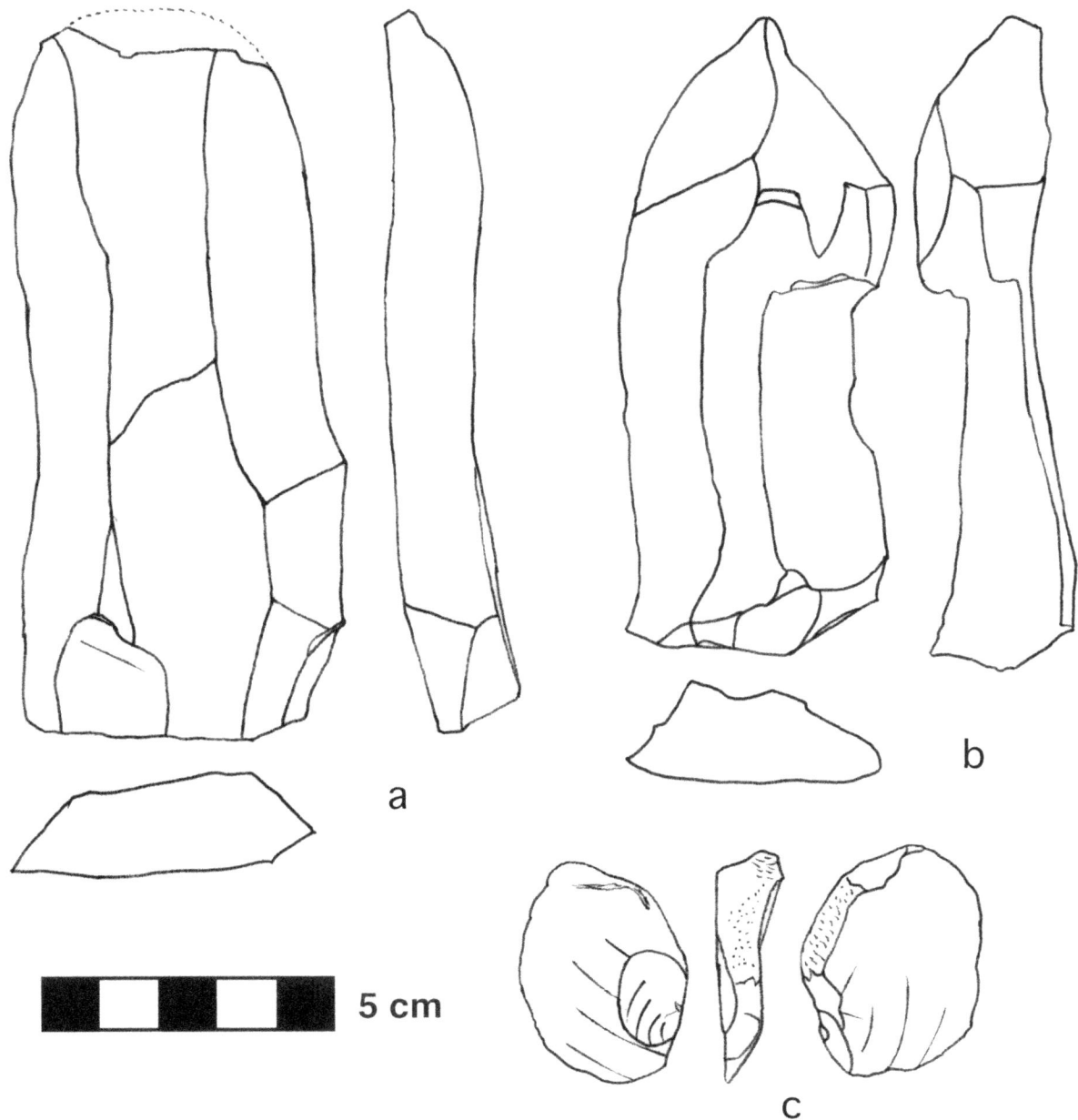

Figure 3.15. Débitage: Special pieces, a-b. large non-Levallois flakes (a. AR99.289, b. AR99.459), c. Kombewa/Janus flake (AR99.256).

dorsal scar pattern (5%). That the majority of flakes from Ar Rasfa are cortical likely reflects the exploitation of nearby raw material sources. The scarcity of relict edges on dorsal flake surfaces is consistent with either minimal core rejuvenation or a greater reliance on radial-centripetal core preparation, which leaves little trace of relict edges.

Of the 1427 artifacts, only 95 (7%) are retouched tools (see Table 3.20). Among technologically-defined tool types, non-Levallois retouched tools are the most common (71%) types of retouched artifacts. Not all of the tools initially classified in 1997 as retouched tools were eventually judged to have been retouched after the imposition of more stringent,

measurement-based criteria in 1999 for identifying retouch (as opposed to large-scale edge-damage) or natural breaks vs. burin scars. Of the other retouched tools, eight are Levallois points, seven are Levallois flakes and five are core-trimming flakes. The percentage of Levallois points that exhibit retouch is between three and four times that of other Levallois products and nearly twice the rate for artifacts overall. This suggests that Levallois points were a special focus for tool curation by retouch.

(NOTE: Although there is a total of 95 retouched tools it was not possible to make a full set of morphological and technological observations on all of these artifacts. Some,

Table 3.15 Débitage: Variation in striking platform morphology.

Technological Type	Absent		Cortical		Plain		Dihedral		Facetted		Other		Total	
	n	%	n	%	n	%	n	%	n	%	n	%	n	%
Levallois Point	2	1		0	3	1		0	56	7		0	61	4
Levallois Blade		0		0	1	0		0	33	4		0	34	2
Levallois Flake	4	1		0	1	0	1	3	172	21	1	10	179	13
Core-Trimming Flake	8	3	1	2	15	7	4	14	52	6		0	80	6
Naturally-Backed Flake		0		0	1	0		0	6	1		0	7	0
Whole Flake	77	24	43	88	152	76	17	59	375	46	6	60	670	47
Retouched Tool	36	11	1	2	2	1	2	7	66	8	1	10	108	8
Non-Proximal Flake Fragment	175	55		0	11	5	2	7	7	1		0	195	14
Proximal Flake Fragment	6	2	4	8	15	7	3	10	49	6	2	20	79	6
Blocky Fragment	10	3		0		0		0		0		0	10	1
Total	318	100	49	100	201	100	29	100	816	100	10	100	1423	100
%	22		3		14		2		57		1		100	

Table 3.16 Débitage: Variation in cortex extent.

Technological Type	None		1-33%		34-66%		67-100%		Indet.		Total	
	n	%	n	%	n	%	n	%	n	%	n	%
Levallois Point	48	7	10	3	2	1	1	1		0	61	4
Levallois Blade	17	2	9	3	7	3	1	1		0	34	2
Levallois Flake	110	16	40	12	23	10	6	4		0	179	13
Core-Trimming Flake	32	5	25	7	16	7	7	5		0	80	6
Naturally-Backed Flake		0	7	2		0		0		0	7	0
Whole Flake	253	36	168	49	144	61	104	76	1	100	670	47
Retouched Tool	66	9	26	8	16	7		0		0	108	8
Non-Proximal Flake Fragment	125	18	41	12	19	8	13	10		0	198	14
Proximal Flake Fragment	49	7	16	5	10	4	4	3		0	79	6
Blocky Fragment	6	1	3	1	1	0		0		0	10	1
Total	706	100	345	100	238	100	136	100	1	100	1426	100
%	50		24		17		10		0		100	

for example, were missing striking platforms. Others had been so modified that technological landmarks could not be identified. For these reasons, the total number of artifacts differs somewhat from table to table.)

b. Débitage Measurements

Descriptive statistics for flake maximum length are shown on Table 3.21. Levallois blades exhibit the longest average value (68.0 mm). These are followed (in descending order) by naturally backed flakes, Levallois points, Levallois flakes, and core-trimming flakes. These longest artifact types, which in principle have more potential utility than shorter tools, are relatively few in number. This pattern could suggest that relatively longer tools were preferentially selected for use or transport off-site.

The highest mean values for technological flake length are for Levallois blades, followed by naturally backed flakes, and Levallois points. Levallois tools are more variable in length values than non-Levallois tools (see Table 3.22).

In term of maximum width, Levallois flakes, core-trimming flakes, retouched tools and whole flakes are about equal on average, and they have the highest maximum width values among detached pieces (see Table 3.23). As monitored by standard deviation values, there do not appear to be great contrasts between Levallois and non-Levallois flakes, except for categories represented by small numbers of artifacts (i.e., naturally-backed flakes and blocky fragments).

Maximum thickness is highest on average among blocky fragments (17.2 mm) (see Table 3.24). Next thickest are

Table 3.17 Débitage: Variation in distal-proximal symmetry.

Technological Type	Proximal		Medial		Distal		Even		Indet.		Total	
n/%	n	%	n	%	n	%	n	%	n	%	n	%
Levallois Point	36	7	6	2	8	3	10	4	1	5	61	5
Levallois Blade	8	2	7	2	11	5	8	3		0	34	3
Levallois Flake	69	13	41	13	24	10	45	17		0	179	13
Core-Trimming Flake	28	5	18	6	21	9	13	5		0	80	6
Naturally-Backed Flake		0	1	0	2	1	4	2		0	7	1
Whole Flake	291	56	185	59	106	46	87	33	1	5	670	50
Retouched Tool	28	5	21	7	24	10	23	9	3	14	99	7
Non-Proximal Flake Fragment	41	8	24	8	29	13	50	19	12	55	156	12
Proximal Flake Fragment	19	4	12	4	5	2	23	9	1	5	60	4
Blocky Fragment	1	0		0		0		0	4	18	5	0
Total	521	100	315	100	230	100	263	100	22	100	1351	100
%	39		23		17		19		2		100	

Table 3.18 Débitage: Variation in medio-lateral symmetry.

Technological Type	Right		Center		Left		Even		Indet.		Total	
	n	%	n	%	n	%	n	%	n	%	n	%
Levallois Point	2	1	46	6	3	1	10	8		0	61	4
Levallois Blade	6	3	23	3	5	2		0		0	34	2
Levallois Flake	18	9	103	13	16	6	41	33	1	7	179	13
Core-Trimming Flake	16	8	29	4	29	12	6	5		0	80	6
Naturally-Backed Flake		0	1	0	6	2		0		0	7	1
Whole Flake	107	56	402	50	126	50	33	27	1	7	669	48
Retouched Tool	11	6	60	7	21	8	11	9	1	7	104	8
Non-Proximal Flake Fragment	21	11	96	12	38	15	11	9	6	43	172	12
Proximal Flake Fragment	10	5	44	5	8	3	11	9	1	7	74	5
Blocky Fragment		0	1	0		0		0	4	29	5	0
Total	191	100	805	100	252	100	123	100	14	100	1385	100
%	14		58		18		9		1		100	

core-trimming flakes (14.8 mm), followed by whole flakes (13.2 mm). Levallois tools are relatively thin compared to non-Levallois tools. Thicker tools consume more raw materials, and have less potential utility than thinner ones, all other things being equal (Davis 2000, Shea et al. 2007). To the extent that flake thickness monitors potential utility, these data suggest that Levallois tools recover cutting edge more efficiently than non-Levallois tools. Standard deviation values of maximum thickness for Levallois tools and non-Levallois tools are about equal; however, suggesting there is much variability in both Levallois and non-Levallois core reduction.

The striking platforms of Levallois points are widest among the morphological tool types (see Table 3.25). The values of striking platform width, though variable, are more-or-less the same for the other morphological tool types. Striking platforms are rarely retouched in Levantine Mousterian

assemblages, which could explain the minimal differences (similar standard deviation values) among these tool types.

In terms of striking platform thickness, flake fragments, core-trimming flakes, retouched tools and whole flakes all show about equal values, 6.3-8.0 mm on average (see Table 3.26). This lack of variation probably reflects a degree of standardization in knapping practices and the mechanical limits of fracture formation.

Proximal flake fragments show the highest mean midpoint width among detached pieces (see Table 3.27). The next widest are Levallois flakes, retouched tools, flake fragments and whole flakes, whose values are about the same. On average, Levallois flakes and non-Levallois flakes are about equally variable with respect to midpoint width.

The highest average values of midpoint thickness are

Table 3.19 Débitage: Variation in dorsal surface morphology.

Technological Tool Type	AC	PCD	PCR	PCL	RED	RER	REL	UDP	UDC	RC	BC	I/O	n
Levallois Point	1		1	1		1		4	31	7	10	5	61
Levallois Blade		2	3	2	1			7	2		14	3	34
Levallois Flake	2	11	12	18	1	1		45	7	31	40	11	179
Core-Trimming Flake	4	6	6	15	6	12	7	10	2	6	5	1	80
Naturally-Backed Flake		2	2	1		1				1			7
Whole Flake	122	73	116	98	2	8	6	76	14	40	61	54	670
Retouched Tool	7	12	7	7	3	3	4	13	7	9	18	18	108
Non-Proximal Flake Fragment	38	17	22	21	1	1	1	9	1	16	23	48	198
Proximal Flake Fragment	6	2	13	13		1	1	17	2	4	2	18	79
Blocky Fragment	2						1					7	10
Total	182	125	182	176	14	28	20	181	66	114	173	165	1426
%	13	9	13	12	1	2	1	13	5	8	12	12	100

KEY: AC = all cortical, PCD = partly cortical distal, PCR= partly cortical right, PCL= partly cortical left, RED = Relict edge distal, RER = Relict edge right, REL = Relict edge left, UDP = Unidirectional-parallel flake scars, UDC = Unidirectional-convergent flake scars, RC = Radial-centripetal flake scars, BC = Bidirectional-Centripetal Flake Scars, I/O = Indet./Other.

Table 3.20 Débitage: Retouched tools among technological types.

Technological Type	Total	Retouched	% Retouched
Levallois Point	61	8	13
Levallois Blade	34	1	3
Levallois Flake	179	7	4
Core-Trimming Flake	80	5	6
Naturally-Backed Flake	7		0
Whole Flake	669		0
Retouched Tool	104	74	71
Non-Proximal Flake Fragment	172		0
Proximal Flake Fragment	74		0
Blocky Fragment	5		0
Total	1385	95	7

those for core-trimming flakes, whole flakes, and proximal flake fragments (see Table 3.28). Levallois tools are systematically thinner at their midpoint than non-Levallois flakes (8-10 mm vs. 10-11 mm).

Retouched Tools

Figures 3.16-3.19 show drawings of selected retouched tools from Ar Rasfa. These include points (Figures 3.16), scrapers (Figure 3.17), and various other types, such as notches, perforators, and unusually large pieces (Figures 3.18-3.19).

Most retouched tools in Mousterian assemblages are retouched unifacially on their dorsal face (Bordes 1961). Burins are characterized by a special kind of retouch that removes portions of both dorsal and ventral faces simultaneously (Bordes 1961, Debénath and Dibble 1994, Inizan et al. 1999). Table 3.29 lists the total number of

artifacts representing different retouched tool types in the Ar Rasfa assemblage. There are approximately even numbers of truncations (n =16), sidescrapers (n = 15), and notches (n =15) in the Ar Rasfa assemblage. These three tool types account for 48% of all the retouched tools. There are also significant numbers of transverse scrapers (n =11).

a. Retouched Tool Attributes

"Whole" flakes are the most technological common types among retouched tools. These and proximal flake fragments account for the majority (65%) of Ar Rasfa retouched tool types (see Table 3.30).

The prominence of proximal flake fragments may reflect the fact that they represent the thickest part of the tool, the easiest part to grasp, and thus (probably) the last part of any tool to be retouched/resharpened. Nevertheless, many retouched flakes lack striking platforms (see Table

Table 3.21 Débitage: Variation in flake maximum length (mm).

Technological Type	Mean	SD	Max.	Min.	n
Levallois Point	59.0	22.7	153	29	61
Levallois Blade	68.0	24.1	130	31	34
Levallois Flake	59.3	20.1	132	26	179
Core-Trimming Flake	59.9	18.0	101	30	80
Naturally-Backed Flake	64.1	12.3	85	48	7
Whole Flake	56.4	19.7	125	18	670
Retouched Tool	54.5	14.5	85	20	108
Non-Proximal Flake Fragment	49.3	17.1	130	17	198
Proximal Flake Fragment	43.7	14.1	90	18	79
Blocky Fragment	41.2	13.7	67	30	9
Total	55.5	19.4	153	17	1425

Table 3.22 Débitage: Variation in flake technological length (mm).

Technological Type	Mean	SD	Max.	Min.	n
Levallois Point	58.9	22.5	153	29	60
Levallois Blade	67.6	23.9	130	31	34
Levallois Flake	56.3	20.9	132	21	178
Core-Trimming Flake	55.5	17.9	95	26	79
Naturally-Backed Flake	62.9	13.6	85	48	7
Whole Flake	52.1	20.1	125	12	668
Retouched Tool	50.6	16.3	85	20	88
Non-Proximal Flake Fragment	44.3	15.7	88	14	117
Proximal Flake Fragment	40.1	16.3	87	2	49
Blocky Fragment	43.7	20.2	67	32	3
Total	52.4	20.1	153	2	1283

Table 3.23 Débitage: Variation in flake maximum width (mm).

Technological Type	Mean	SD	Max.	Min.	n
Levallois Point	38.3	12.2	73	12	61
Levallois Blade	32.5	17.0	115	14	34
Levallois Flake	41.6	13.2	87	2	179
Core-Trimming Flake	41.4	15.3	83	15	80
Naturally-Backed Flake	33.9	4.2	40	29	7
Whole Flake	40.1	14.2	108	14	670
Retouched Tool	41.9	12.8	72	15	108
Non-Proximal Flake Fragment	35.9	13.5	93	13	196
Proximal Flake Fragment	36.7	12.1	86	18	79
Blocky Fragment	27.5	3.8	32	21	10
Total	39.3	13.9	115	2	1424

Table 3.24 Débitage: Variation in flake maximum thickness (mm).

Technological Type	Mean	SD	Max.	Min.	n
Levallois Point	10.0	6.1	45	4	61
Levallois Blade	10.9	4.3	20	4	34
Levallois Flake	10.5	5.9	60	3	179
Core-Trimming Flake	14.2	5.7	31	5	80
Naturally-Backed Flake	10.0	2.0	12	7	7
Whole Flake	13.2	5.7	47	3	670
Retouched Tool	12.6	5.1	36	5	108
Non-Proximal Flake Fragment	11.4	5.4	41	4	198
Proximal Flake Fragment	10.5	4.4	30	5	79
Blocky Fragment	17.2	7.0	25	7	10
Total	12.3	5.7	60	3	1426

Table 3.25 Débitage: Variation in striking platform width by technological types (mm).

Technological Type	Mean	SD	Max.	Min.	n
Levallois Point	31.9	11.5	67	9	60
Levallois Blade	18.9	6.3	36	8	34
Levallois Flake	25.9	11.6	83	5	176
Core-Trimming Flake	21.6	11.9	58	4	75
Naturally-Backed Flake	19.3	5.2	29	14	7
Whole Flake	21.0	11.8	108	1	605
Retouched Tool	26.9	12.8	63	5	69
Non-Proximal Flake Fragment	21.5	7.4	36	8	15
Proximal Flake Fragment	21.2	9.2	50	4	71
Blocky Fragment					
Total	22.7	11.9	108	1	1112

Table 3.26 Débitage: Variation in striking platform thickness (mm).

Technological Type	Mean	SD	Max.	Min.	n
Levallois Point	6.4	1.9	11	3	60
Levallois Blade	6.3	2.5	16	3	34
Levallois Flake	6.9	4.0	41	2	175
Core-Trimming Flake	7.9	3.2	23	3	75
Naturally-Backed Flake	6.0	2.0	8	2	7
Whole Flake	7.7	4.1	31	1	605
Retouched Tool	7.8	4.7	26	2	70
Non-Proximal Flake Fragment	8.0	2.8	12	4	15
Proximal Flake Fragment	6.7	3.0	19	2	71
Blocky Fragment					
Total	7.4	3.9	41	1	1112

Table 3.27 Débitage: Variation in midpoint width (mm).

Technological Type	Mean	SD	Max.	Min.	n
Levallois Point	34.4	11.2	63	8	51
Levallois Blade	27.9	7.6	46	14	31
Levallois Flake	39.2	11.7	67	3	140
Core-Trimming Flake	36.9	13.5	75	10	72
Naturally-Backed Flake	32.0	4.9	40	24	7
Whole Flake	37.6	13.3	108	13	491
Retouched Tool	38.2	10.8	63	11	50
Non-Proximal Flake Fragment	37.7	5.4	47	32	6
Proximal Flake Fragment	40.9	12.1	72	27	14
Blocky Fragment					
Total	37.3	12.7	108	3	862

Table 3.28 Débitage: Variation in flake midpoint thickness (mm).

Technological Type	Mean	SD	Max.	Min.	n
Levallois Point	8.1	4.1	29	3	51
Levallois Blade	9.2	3.5	18	3	31
Levallois Flake	8.3	3.2	18	3	140
Core-Trimming Flake	11.1	4.5	24	4	72
Naturally-Backed Flake	7.6	2.0	10	5	7
Whole Flake	11.2	5.0	35	2	490
Retouched Tool	10.6	7.1	50	4	50
Non-Proximal Flake Fragment	10.8	3.7	18	6	8
Proximal Flake Fragment	11.3	5.6	29	6	15
Blocky Fragment					
Total	10.4	4.9	50	2	864

Table 3.29 Count of retouched tool types.

Retouched Tool Type	n	%
1. Transverse Scraper	11	11.6
2. Sidescraper	15	15.8
3. Backed Knife	3	3.2
4. Notch	15	15.8
5. Denticulate	8	8.4
6. Awl	3	3.2
7. Burin	6	6.3
8. Truncation	16	16.8
9. Combination tool	8	8.4
10. Other	8	8.4
11. Retouched Levallois Point	2	2.1
Total	95	100.0

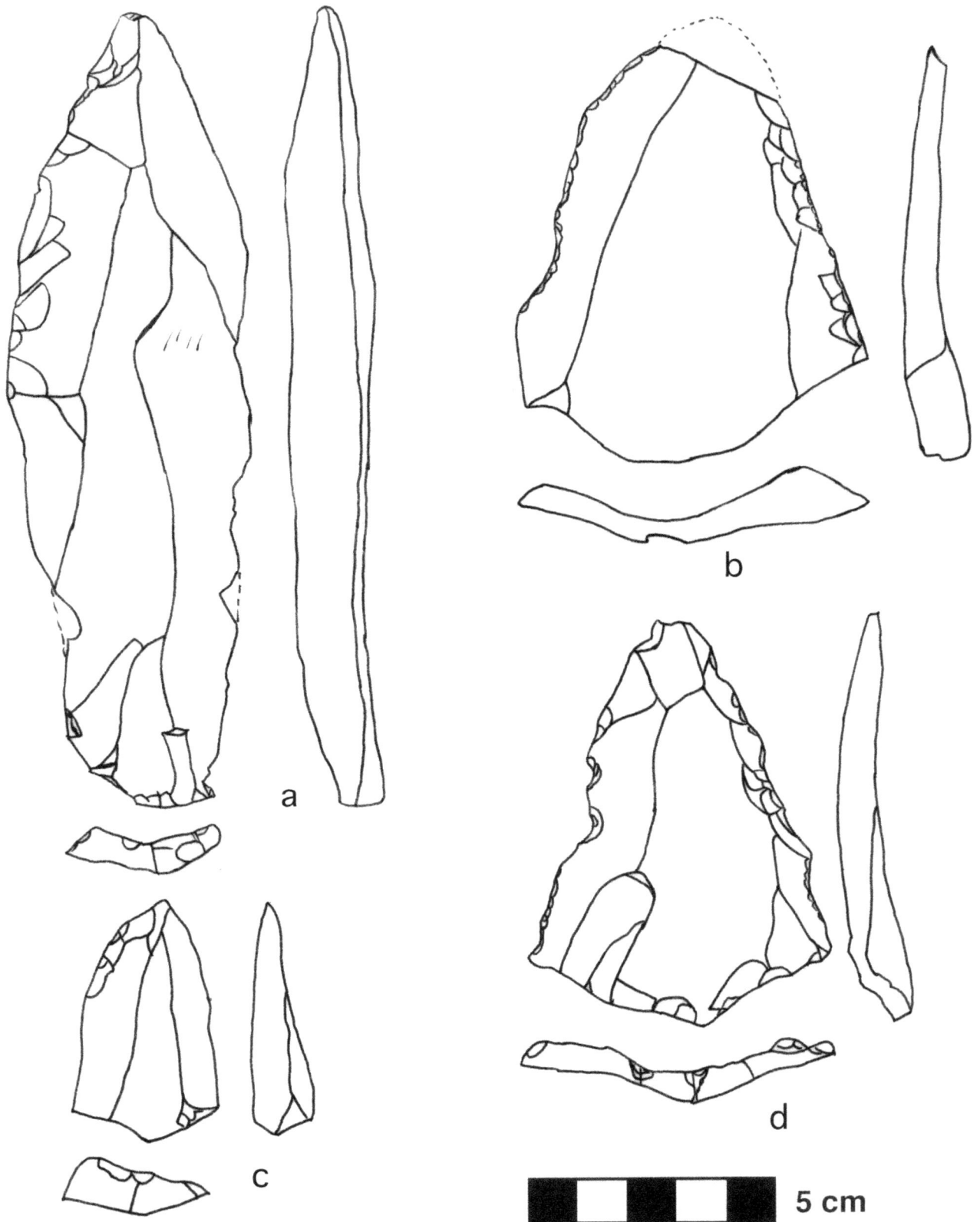

Figure 3.16. Retouched Tools: Points, a. elongated, retouched Levallois point (Abu Sif knife)(AR97.155), b-d. retouched Levallois points (b. AR97.120, c. AR99.24, d. AR97.214).

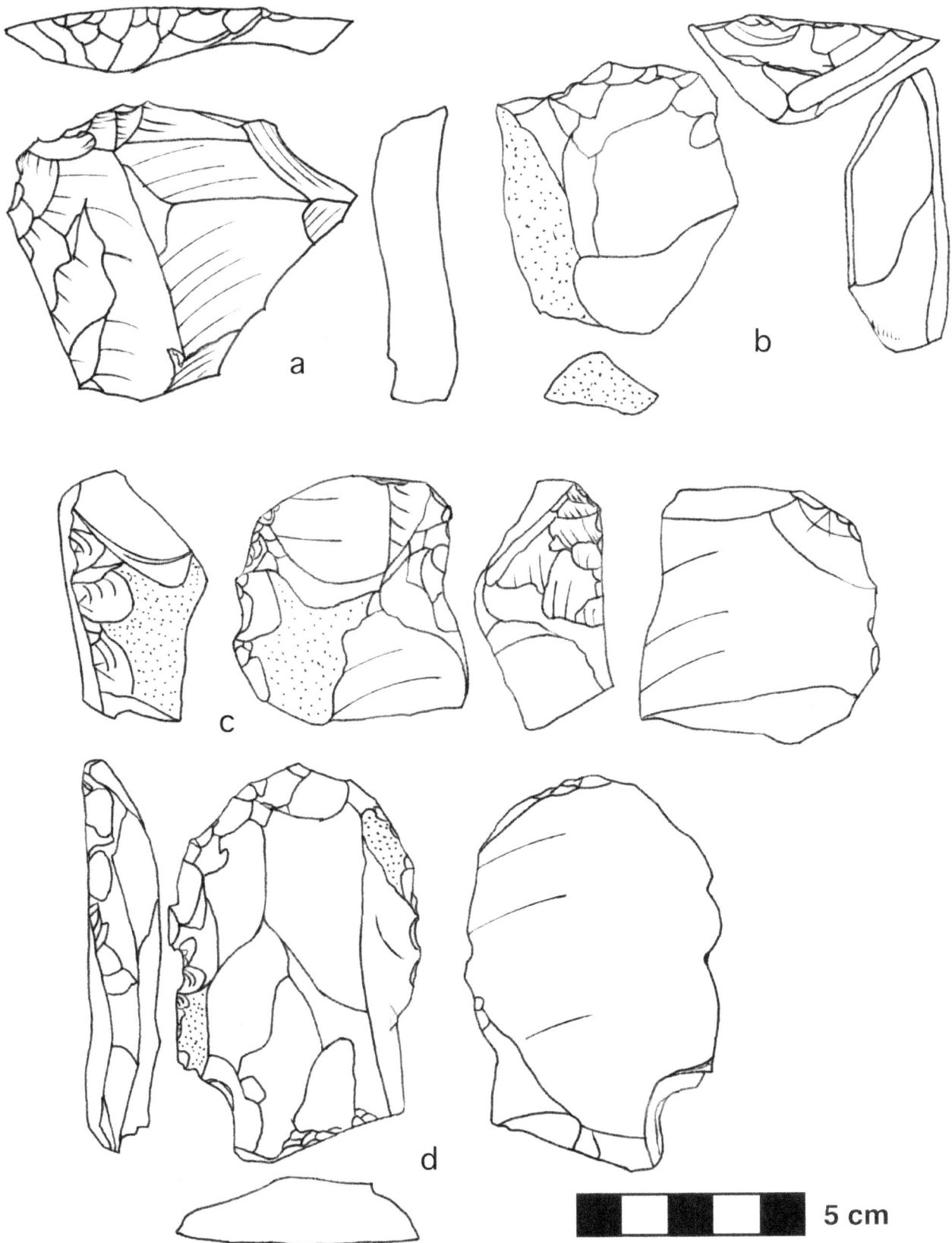

Figure 3.17. Retouched Tools: Scrapers a. transverse scraper (AR99.17), b. end-retouched piece (AR99.252), c. double sidescraper (AR99.163), d. complex scraper (AR99.322).

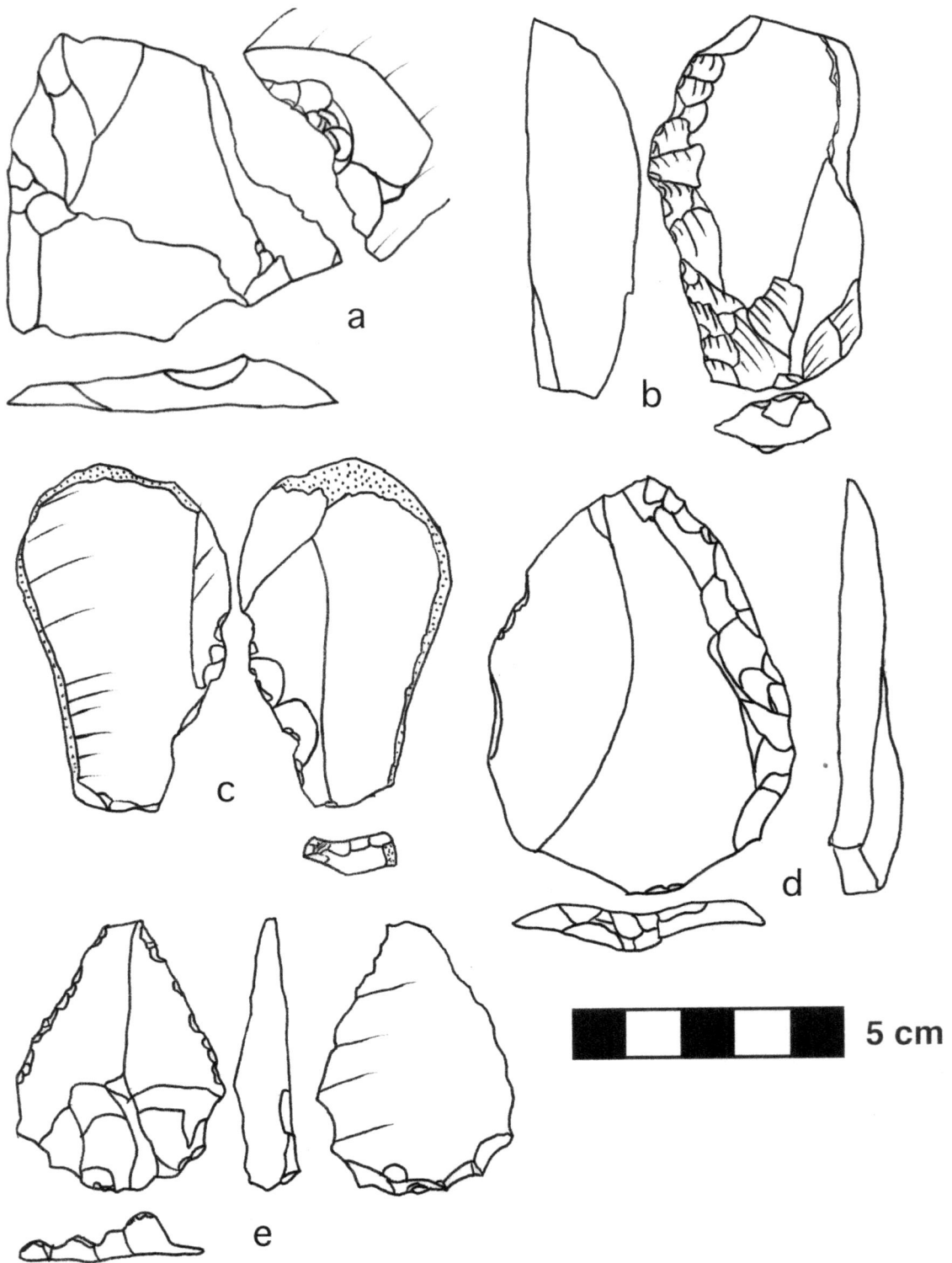

Figure 3.18. Retouched Tools: Other retouched tools, a. notch (AR97.168), b. sidescraper (AR97.159), c. denticulate (AR97.111), d. point/sidescraper (AR97.47), e. point with basal modification (AR97.10).

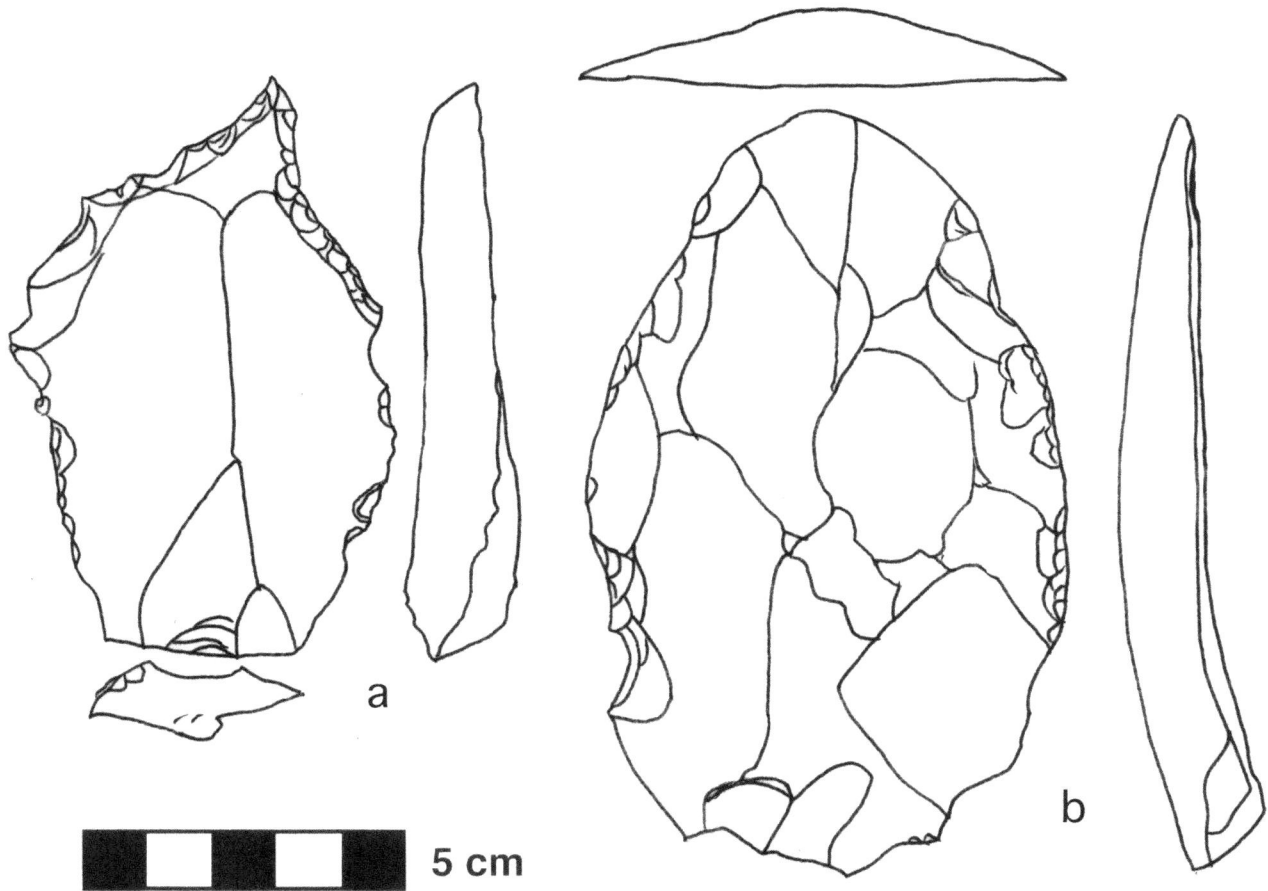

Figure 3.19. Retouched Tools: Large retouched tools, a. perforator (AR97.89), b. large retouched Levallois flake with basal thinning (AR97.146).

Table 3.30 Retouched Tools: Count of completeness

Retouched Tool Type	Whole Flake		Proximal Flake Fragment		Medial Flake Fragment		Distal Flake Fragment	
	n	%	n	%	n	%	n	%
Transverse Scraper	5	12	4	21	2	14		0
Sidescraper	9	21	1	5	2	14	3	23
Backed Knife	3	7		0		0		0
Notch	9	21	2	11		0	3	23
Denticulate	3	7	2	11	2	14	1	8
Awl	2	5		0		0		0
Burin	2	5	1	5	1	7	2	15
Truncation	4	9	3	16	6	43	2	15
Combination Tool	3	7	2	11		0		0
Retouched Levallois Point	2	5		0		0		0
Other	1	2	4	21	1	7	2	15
Total	43	100	19	100	14	100	13	100
%	45		20		15		14	

Table 3.30 Continued.

Retouched Tool Type	Lateral Flake Fragment		Blocky Fragment		Other		Total	
	n	%	n	%	n	%	n	%
Transverse Scraper		0		0		0	11	12
Sidescraper		0		0		0	15	16
Backed Knife		0		0		0	3	3
Notch		0		0	1	25	15	16
Denticulate		0		0		0	8	8
Awl		0		0	1	25	3	3
Burin		0		0		0	6	6
Truncation		0	1	100		0	16	17
Combination Tool	1	100		0	2	50	8	8
Retouched Levallois Point		0		0		0	2	2
Other		0		0		0	8	8
Total	1	100	1	100	4	100	95	100
%	1		1		4		100	

Table 3.31 Retouched Tools: Variation in striking platform morphology.

Retouched Tool Type	Absent		Cortical		Plain		Facetted		Dihedral		Other		Total	
	n	%	n	%	n	%	n	%	n	%	n	%	n	%
Transverse Scraper	4	11	1	100		0	6	12		0		0	11	12
Sidescraper	6	16		0		0	8	16	1	50		0	15	16
Backed Knife		0		0		0	3	6		0		0	3	3
Notch	4	11		0	1	50	9	18	1	50		0	15	16
Denticulate	3	8		0		0	5	10		0		0	8	8
Awl	1	3		0		0	2	4		0		0	3	3
Burin	2	5		0		0	3	6		0	1	100	6	6
Truncation	13	34		0		0	3	6		0		0	16	17
Combination Tool	3	8		0	1	50	4	8		0		0	8	8
Retouched Levallois Point		0		0		0	2	4		0		0	2	2
Other	2	5		0		0	6	12		0		0	8	8
Total	38	100	1	100	2	100	51	100	2	100	1	100	95	100
%	40		1		2		54		2		1		100	

3.31). Of the 54% of the retouched tools preserving striking platforms, 51 (90%) have facetted striking platforms. This pattern is similar to that for flakes and flake fragments, again suggesting an emphasis on careful core preparation.

Most retouched tools have no cortex on the dorsal surface (see Table 3.32); none has more than 66% cortex. Tools with less than 33% cortex amount to 87% of retouched tools from Ar-Rasfa. Cortex is a relatively ineffective material for use as a cutting edge, and thus the predominance of non-cortical and minimally-cortical flakes among retouched tools may suggest a rational preference for tool blanks that had the maximum amount of useful, non-cortical mass.

Most retouched flakes (59%) are even along their entire length or thickest at the proximal end (see Table 3.33). Nevertheless, a substantial number of retouched tools are thickest medially, or at their distal end. Following the basic evolutionary principle that relaxed selection increases variability (Gould and Lewontin 1979), the lack of a clear pattern of preference, or standardization of blank shape suggests a fairly casual, non-selective approach to blank selection.

Sixty-two percent of all retouched tools are thickest at the center of their medio-lateral plane (see Table 3.34). The next highest percentage is thickest at the left lateral edge (15%). This pattern seems to suggest a pattern of

Table 3.32 Retouched Tools: Variation in cortex extent.

Retouched Tool Type	None		1-33%		34-66%		>66%		Total	
	n	%	n	%	n	%	n	%	n	%
Transverse Scraper	5	8	6	29		0			11	12
Sidescraper	10	16	2	10	3	25			15	16
Backed Knife	1	2	1	5	1	8			3	3
Notch	9	15	4	19	2	17			15	16
Denticulate	5	8		0	3	25			8	8
Awl	2	3	1	5		0			3	3
Burin	5	8	1	5		0			6	6
Truncation	13	21	2	10	1	8			16	17
Combination Tool	4	6	2	10	2	17			8	8
Retouched Levallois Point	2	3		0		0			2	2
Other	6	10	2	10		0			8	8
Total	62	100	21	100	12	100	0		95	100
%	65		22		13		0		100	

Table 3.33 Retouched Tools: Count of distal-proximal symmetry.

Retouched Tool Type	Proximal		Medial		Distal		Even		Other		Total	
	n	%	n	%	n	%	n	%	n	%	n	%
Transverse Scraper	2	8	3	18		0	5	19		0	10	12
Sidescraper	5	20	2	12	2	13	4	15	1	33	14	16
Backed Knife		0	1	6	1	7	1	4		0	3	3
Notch	6	24	3	18	3	20	1	4	1	33	14	16
Denticulate	2	8	2	12	3	20		0		0	7	8
Awl		0	1	6	1	7	1	4		0	3	3
Burin	1	4		0		0	3	12		0	4	5
Truncation	2	8	1	6	2	13	8	31	1	33	14	16
Combination Tool	3	12	1	6	2	13	2	8		0	8	9
Retouched Levallois Point	1	4	1	6		0		0		0	2	2
Other	3	12	2	12	1	7	1	4		0	7	8
Total	25	100	17	100	15	100	26	100	3	100	86	100
%	29		20		17		30		3		100	

selection for medio-lateral symmetry that contrasts with the seemingly-casual selection for blanks based on their distal-proximal symmetry (see above).

Using the original classification of dorsal surface pattern, the three most common patterns are bidirectional-centripetal flake scars, unidirectional-parallel flake scars, and partly cortical right (see Table 3.35). Together, these account for 39% of the retouched tools. This original dorsal surface pattern classification is highly contingent, making it difficult to detect a pattern in the data. A clearer pattern emerges when one collapses some of these dorsal surface contingencies along the following lines: cortical flakes of any kind (all cortical, partially cortical-dorsal, partially cortical-right and partially cortical-left), flakes with relict edges, flakes with unidirectional scarring (unidirectional-parallel and unidirectional- convergent), and flakes with multidirectional scarring (radial/centripetal flake scars and bidirectional-opposed flake scars). Leaving aside the indeterminate specimens (n = 19), the largest percentage of retouched tool dorsal surfaces is cortical (n= 32 or 34%), followed by multidirectional (n = 23 or 24%) and unidirectional (n= 17 or 18%). The predominance of cortical and multidirectional-scarred dorsal surface patterns suggests blanks for retouched tools were being selected from products of the earliest and latest stages of

Table 3.34 Retouched Tools: Variation in medio-lateral symmetry.

Retouched Tool Type	Right		Center		Left		Even		Other		Total	
	n	%	n	%	n	%	n	%	n	%	n	%
Transverse Scraper	1	10	7	13	1	7	2	20		0	11	12
Sidescraper	2	20	9	16	1	7	2	20		0	14	15
Backed Knife	1	10	2	4		0		0		0	3	3
Notch	1	10	11	20		0	1	10	1	100	14	15
Denticulate	1	10	3	5	4	29		0		0	8	9
Awl		0	1	2	1	7	1	10		0	3	3
Burin		0	4	7	1	7		0		0	5	5
Truncation	3	30	6	11	3	21	3	30		0	15	16
Combination Tool	1	10	4	7	3	21		0		0	8	9
Retouched Levallois Point		0	2	4		0		0		0	2	2
Other		0	7	13		0	1	10		0	8	9
Total	10	100	56	100	14	100	10	100	1	100	91	100
%	11		62		15		11		1		100	

Table 3.35 Retouched Tools: Variation in dorsal surface morphology.

Retouched Tool Type	AC	PCD	PCR	PCL	RED	RER	REL	UDP	UDC	RC	BC	I/O	n
Transverse Scraper	1			1		1		2			3	2	1	11
Sidescraper		3	3					1	3		3	2	15
Backed Knife			2								1		3
Notch	1	3	1		1		1	1	1	1	2	3	15
Denticulate	2		1	1				1				3	8
Awl								1			1	1	3
Burin			1					2			1	2	6
Truncation		2	1	1		1		1		5	4	1	16
Combination Tool	2	1	2	1								2	8
Retouched Levallois Point								1				1	2
Other	1		1					2	1			3	8
Total	7	9	11	5	1	2	1	12	5	9	14	19	95
%	7	9	12	5	1	2	1	13	5	9	15	20	100

KEY: AC = all cortical, PCD = partly cortical distal, PCR= partly cortical right, PCL= partly cortical left, RED = Relict edge distal, RER = Relict edge right, REL = Relict edge left, UDP = Unidirectional-parallel flake scars, UDC = Unidirectional-convergent flake scars, RC = Radial-centripetal flake scars, BC = Bidirectional-Centripetal Flake Scars, I/O = Indet./Other.

core reduction. This could suggest that tools produced in the middle phases of core reduction, i.e., blanks with unidirectional scars and blanks with relict edges, were being selected for transport and use elsewhere. Such tools are large and would, in principle, possess considerable potential utility. One would not expect them to have been systematically overlooked in selection for use.

In terms of their location, most retouched edges are on the distal end of flakes (68%) or on the right lateral edge (25%)(see Table 3.36). That few tools show retouch on the proximal end is not particularly surprising, but the near-absence of retouch on left lateral edges is striking. Traditional lithic typologies do not differentiate between tools with retouch on right vs. left lateral edges (Bisson 2000). Thus, it is difficult to say if this preference for retouching right lateral edges over left lateral edges at Ar Rasfa is common or if it is unusual in Levantine Mousterian assemblages.

Table 3.36 Retouched Tools: Distribution of retouched edges on retouched tools.

Retouched Tool Type	Distal		Right Lateral		Proximal		Left Lateral		Total	
	n	%	n	%	n	%	n	%	n	%
Transverse Scraper	8	13	2	9		0	1	100	11	12
Sidescraper	13	21	2	9		0		0	15	16
Backed Knife	2	3	1	4		0		0	3	3
Notch	13	21	1	4	1	17		0	15	16
Denticulate	7	11	1	4		0		0	8	9
Awl	1	2	2	9		0		0	3	3
Burin	4	6	1	4	1	17		0	6	6
Truncation	7	11	7	30	2	33		0	16	17
Combination Tool	4	6	2	9	2	33		0	8	9
Retouched Levallois Point		0		0		0		0		0
Other	4	6	4	17		0		0	8	9
Total	63	100	23	100	6	100	1	100	93	100
%	68		25		6		1		100	

Table 3.37 Retouched Tools: Variation in maximum length (mm).

Retouched Tool Type	Mean	SD	Max.	Min.	n
Transverse Scraper	55.0	19.1	87	32	11
Sidescraper	60.7	14.6	85	37	15
Backed Knife	73.7	27.6	93	42	3
Notch	56.5	15.7	80	33	15
Denticulate	46.0	9.6	60	33	8
Awl	54.3	11.7	67	44	3
Burin	51.2	20.8	80	20	6
Truncation	55.7	14.9	83	35	16
Combination Tool	56.0	12.6	72	33	8
Retouched Levallois Point	107.5	64.3	153	62	2
Other	44.3	13.5	71	30	8
Total	56.1	18.8	153	20	95

Table 3.38 Retouched Tools: Variation in technological length (mm).

Retouched Tool Type	Mean	SD	Max.	Min.	n
Transverse Scraper	47.1	20.0	87	23	8
Sidescraper	60.5	15.4	85	34	12
Backed Knife	73.7	27.6	93	42	3
Notch	49.5	15.3	79	22	14
Denticulate	40.3	13.8	60	24	6
Awl	48.7	4.2	52	44	3
Burin	46.3	25.0	80	20	4
Truncation	56.0	21.4	83	24	10
Combination Tool	52.0	7.0	65	43	7
Retouched Levallois Point	107.5	64.3	153	62	2
Other	36.3	15.3	64	21	6
Total	52.6	21.4	153	20	75

Retouched Tool Measurements

In terms of maximum length (see Table 3.37) and technological length (see Table 3.38), retouched Levallois points have the greatest average values, and they show the most variation among retouched tool types. The next longest retouched tool category, on average, is backed knives.

Maximum width is greatest among combination tools and notches (see Table 3.39). Awls are the next widest, on average. Awls exhibit greatest variation in maximum width among retouched tool types.

In terms of maximum thickness, notches and combination tools preserve the highest mean values, followed by denticulates (see Table 3.40). The next thickest average values are about equal for transverse scrapers, backed knives, awls, sidescrapers, truncations and retouched points. In terms of standard deviation, all variables except

notches are about equal. Only burins are noticeably thinner on average.

The highest average value of striking platform width among retouched tool types is for sidescrapers (see Table 3.41). The second highest average value on average is for retouched Levallois points. Sidescrapers show the greatest variation in striking platform width, followed by denticulates and truncations, whose values are similar to one another.

The greatest average values for striking platform width are for awls and denticulates (see Table 3.42). The next-highest values are for notches. Denticulates exhibit much greater variation in striking platform width than other retouch tools.

The greatest average value of midpoint width is for awls (see Table 3.43). The second and third widest are truncations and combination tools, which have similar values.

Transverse scrapers have the highest mean values of midpoint thickness among entire retouched tool types (see

Table 3.39. Retouched Tools: Variation in maximum width (mm).

Retouched Tool Type	Mean	SD	Max.	Min.	n
Transverse Scraper	44.8	13.3	70	26	11
Sidescraper	44.4	14.2	67	21	15
Backed Knife	35.0	12.5	45	21	3
Notch	48.1	13.5	71	22	15
Denticulate	36.9	8.8	49	22	8
Awl	47.7	21.6	68	25	3
Burin	31.5	14.0	50	18	6
Truncation	42.9	8.7	57	29	16
Combination Tool	49.3	11.8	57	21	8
Retouched Levallois Point	40.0	8.5	46	34	2
Other	40.3	12.1	55	21	8
Total	43.1	12.8	71	18	95

Table 3.40 Retouched Tools: Variation in maximum thickness (mm).

Retouched Tool Type	Mean	SD	Max.	Min.	n
Transverse Scraper	12.8	4.4	21	7	11
Sidescraper	12.5	5.9	24	5	15
Backed Knife	12.7	5.5	18	7	3
Notch	15.4	7.1	36	8	15
Denticulate	14.5	5.8	23	7	8
Awl	12.7	4.5	17	8	3
Burin	9.5	3.0	14	5	6
Truncation	11.6	2.7	16	7	16
Combination Tool	15.4	3.6	19	10	8
Retouched Levallois Point	11.0	4.2	14	8	2
Other	12.9	4.7	21	7	8
Total	13.1	5.1	36	5	95

Table 3.41 Retouched Tools: Variation in striking platform width (mm).

Retouched Tool Type	Mean	SD	Max.	Min.	n
Transverse Scraper	20.3	7.4	28	5	7
Sidescraper	32.1	18.7	67	14	9
Backed Knife	19.3	3.2	23	17	3
Notch	24.4	13.1	42	7	11
Denticulate	25.2	15.6	44	10	5
Awl	24.5	7.8	30	19	2
Burin	23.0	11.3	31	15	2
Truncation	20.0	15.6	31	9	2
Combination Tool	22.8	7.7	36	18	5
Retouched Levallois Point	30.0	5.7	34	26	2
Other	30.8	10.3	43	18	6
Total	25.5	12.4	67	5	54

Table 3.42 Retouched Tools: Variation in striking platform width (mm).

Retouched Tool Type	Mean	SD	Max.	Min.	n
Transverse Scraper	7.4	3.4	12	2	7
Sidescraper	7.3	3.5	13	3	9
Backed Knife	7.7	1.5	9	6	3
Notch	10.3	5.7	22	3	11
Denticulate	12.2	9.1	26	5	5
Awl	12.5	3.5	15	10	2
Burin	7.0	2.6	9	4	3
Truncation	6.0	0.0	6	6	2
Combination Tool	8.4	3.3	14	6	5
Retouched Levallois Point	7.0	1.4	8	6	2
Other	7.0	1.5	9	5	6
Total	8.6	4.5	26	2	55

Table 3.43 Retouched Tools: Variation in midpoint width (mm).

Retouched Tool Type	Mean	SD	Max.	Min.	n
Transverse Scraper	36.5	17.6	50	11	4
Sidescraper	39.9	7.6	51	27	7
Backed Knife	40.0	1.4	41	39	2
Notch	39.8	15.9	63	20	5
Denticulate	32.5	0.7	33	32	2
Awl	62.0	n.a.	62	62	1
Burin	31.5	24.7	49	14	2
Truncation	50.5	3.5	53	48	2
Combination Tool	48.8	4.6	55	44	4
Retouched Levallois Point	37.5	9.2	44	31	2
Other	34.5	4.9	38	31	2
Total	40.4	11.8	63	11	33

Table 3.44 Retouched Tools: Variation in midpoint thickness (mm).

Retouched Tool Type	Mean	SD	Max.	Min.	n
Transverse Scraper	20.0	20.3	50	6	4
Sidescraper	11.1	3.9	16	7	7
Backed Knife	11.5	0.7	12	11	2
Notch	14.2	7.9	28	9	5
Denticulate	12.0	1.4	13	11	2
Awl	13.0	n.a.	13	13	1
Burin	6.0	2.8	8	4	2
Truncation	12.0	1.4	13	11	2
Combination Tool	12.5	3.7	17	9	4
Retouched Levallois Point	9.5	6.4	14	5	2
Other	7.5	2.1	9	6	2
Total	12.4	8.1	50	4	33

Table 3.45 Retouched Edges: Cross-tabulation of retouched edge shape and retouch mode.

Edge Shape	Dorsal		Ventral		Bifacial		Burin		Alternating		Total	
	n	%	n	%	n	%	n	%	n	%	n	%
Point	3	4	1	4		0	6	55		0	10	8
Convex	14	18	1	4	5	50		0	1	50	21	17
Straight	14	18	8	31	3	30	3	27	1	50	29	23
Concave	28	36	9	35		0	1	9		0	38	30
Recurved	9	12	6	23	2	20		0		0	17	13
Denticulate	10	13	1	4		0		0		0	11	9
Other		0		0		0	1	9		0	1	1
Total	78	100	26	100	10	100	11	100	2	100	127	100
%	61		20		8		9		2		100	

Table 3.46 Retouched Edges: Summary statistics for maximum invasiveness and maximum spine-plane angle.

Statistics	Maximum Invasiveness	Maximum Spine-Plane Angle
Mean	11	65
Standard Error	1	1
Median	10	65
Mode	12	60
Standard Deviation	6	16
Sample Variance	38	253
Kurtosis	2	0
Skewness	1	0
Range	31	86
Minimum	2	19
Maximum	33	105
n	128	128

Table 3.44). The next largest values are for notches and awls, which have similar values. Transverse scrapers show the greatest variation in midpoint thickness.

Retouched Edges

Table 3.45 shows a cross-tabulation of Retouched Edge Shape and Retouch Mode. The most common combination of edge shape is concave, and the most common retouch mode is dorsal. The most common combination of edge shape and retouch mode is concave/dorsal (n = 28 or 22%). This is followed by convex/dorsal and straight/dorsal,

together (each n = 14 or 11%). Burination, bifacial retouch, and alternating retouch are relatively uncommon.

The mean maximum invasiveness of retouched edges at Ar Rasfa is 11 mm (SD = 6)(see Table 3.46). The mean spine-plane angle is 65° (SD = 16°). In principle, edges that are more heavily retouched should show high values for both of these variables. At Ar Rasfa, maximum invasiveness and maximum spine-plane angle are neither strongly nor positively correlated with one another ($r^2 = 0.223$, 126 degrees of freedom, p = 0.09).

CHAPTER 4.

ANALYSIS OF LITHIC ARTIFACT VARIABILITY

This chapter focuses on "paleoethnography", reconstructing variation in particular behavioral strategies related to the formation of the Ar Rasfa lithic assemblage. The four major categories of strategies examined include (1) raw material procurement, (2) tool manufacturing, (3) tool use, and (4) discard behavior. For each of these dimensions of technological behavior, this chapter examines how the Ar Rasfa lithic evidence fits into a framework of contrasting strategic extremes. Questions relating to the plausible "cultural" affinities of the Ar Rasfa Middle Paleolithic assemblage will be examined in the Conclusion, Chapter 5.

Raw Material Procurement Strategies

Ethnographic studies of recent stone-tool-using humans show that raw material procurement is a complex process (Binford 1979, Gould 1980, Hayden 1979, Hayden and Nelson 1981, Kuhn 1995). In some cases it involves people going directly to special-purpose quarry sites and transporting raw materials in bulk to manufacturing and/ or habitation sites (Binford 1986, Toth et al. 1992). In other cases, raw material procurement is "embedded" in daily foraging activities (Gould 1980). In still others, raw materials are procured from remote locations by exchange, a "chain of connection" that can stretch hundreds or even thousands of kilometers (Cann et al. 1969, Gould 1980, Whittaker 2004). None of these raw material procurement strategies is mutually-exclusive. Thus, archaeological assemblages may combine the residues of direct, embedded, and exchange-based raw material procurement strategies.

For archaeological studies, such detailed distinctions among raw material procurement strategies are difficult to make, because of sampling issues, time-averaging, and other uncertainties about site formation processes. Instead, most archaeologists model raw material procurement in terms of the use of either local or exotic raw material sources (Feblot-Augustins 1997). By "local," archaeologists usually mean sources within daily foraging ranges (<10-15 kilometers on open, level terrain). "Exotic" sources are those lying beyond daily foraging ranges (>10-15 kilometers). In most cases, local sources are more variable in quality, whereas those from exotic sources are consistently of higher quality. This phenomenon is thought to reflect efforts to optimize energetic returns on the time and/or energy expended in procuring these materials (Odell 2000).

The first step in identifying procurement strategies is to compare the lithic raw materials in an assemblage to those available from local sources. Most such comparisons are based on macroscopic visual assessments of raw material composition, color, texture, and weather conditions. Other geophysical methods, such as petrography, geochemistry, neutron activation analysis, X-ray fluorescence analysis, PIXE, and similar techniques are sometimes used as well, particularly when there are doubts about similar sources distributed over a wide area.

Today, high quality flint is readily abundant at the Ar Rasfa site. The site is located on flint-rich Cenomanian and Turonian limestone exposures. Flint is exposed in limestone cliffs upslope from the Ar Rasfa site, and it is available in the form of small and large (<20-30 cm) nodules in gravel and alluvium deposits in all of the *wadis* and fields around the site. Experimental fracturing of these nodules reveals exceptionally high-quality flint. This material is largely free of significant fossil inclusions and other faults that would be obstacles to knapping. Freshly-exposed surfaces are a light brown to tan or grey color; some specimens feature distinctive sets of light red concentric rings. This flint weathers quickly when exposed to direct sunlight, changing swiftly to a lighter tan and finally white appearance. Visual comparison of the Ar Rasfa lithics as they were being cleaned (by Shea and Crawford) suggests that nearly all of the flint morphologies in the Ar Rasfa assemblage are within the range of variation of flint in local deposits (J. Shea Field Notes 1997-1999),

The second step in identifying procurement strategies is to examine technological variation among stone tools in an assemblage. This provides a more nuanced sense of which strategies were most important for the formation of an assemblage.

If raw material procurement at Ar Rasfa was primarily local, the following hypotheses should be supported.

1. Cortex should be extensive overall, and particularly among larger flakes.
2. On flake dorsal surfaces, cortical and unidirectional flake scar patterns should be more common than radial-centripetal, bidirectional-opposed scar patterns, and more common than flakes with relict core edges on them (core trimming elements).
3. In terms of striking platform morphology, cortical and plain patterns should be more common than dihedral and facetted ones.
4. There being few incentives to economize core surface area near raw material sources, the striking platform width relative to striking platform thickness should show no relationship with flake size (as expressed in the flake surface area/thickness ratio).

These hypotheses were tested using the whole flakes from Ar Rasfa (n = 983). Retouched tools were excluded from this comparison because the original states of their dorsal surface and/or striking platforms could not be ascertained. Flake fragments were excluded to avoid double-counting the same artifacts.

In assessing the relationship between cortex extent and flake length and to simplify the comparison, cortex extent values were reconfigured into minimally-cortical flakes (<66% of dorsal surface) and predominantly-cortical flakes (>66% of dorsal surface). Length values for these different cortical flake types were compared and found to differ at a high level of statistical significance (t = 6.94, df = 556, p <.01). In terms of their technological length, minimally-cortical flakes are significantly shorter (mean = 51 mm, SD = 20, n = 676) than predominantly-cortical flakes (mean = 61, SD =21, n = 303)(see Table 4.1 and Figure 4.1). These data support the hypothesis of local raw material procurement at Ar Rasfa.

In terms of dorsal surface morphology, the Ar Rasfa data conform to expectations for local raw material procurement (Table 4.2). To examine these data, the dorsal surface patterns for whole flakes were cross-tabulated against groups of flakes sorted by technological length (< 50 mm, 51-100 mm, and >100 mm). In all size categories cortical flakes outnumber non-cortical ones, and they significantly outnumber flakes with relict edges on them. Somewhat surprisingly, unidirectional flakes, which one might reasonably expect to predominate over multidirectional ones in the initial stages of core reduction and with local tool production, do not outnumber flakes with multidirectional scars.

One plausible explanation for the numerical parity between flakes with unidirectional and multidirectional dorsal surface scar patterning may be that larger flakes with unidirectional scars on them were preferentially selected for use and/or transport. To investigate this possibility, dorsal scar patterns of retouched tools were examined (Table 4.3). Among retouched tools, unidirectional dorsal surface scarring patterns are not more common than multidirectional ones, but they are significantly more common overall, proportionately, than among whole flakes (chi-square = 32.4, df = 1, p <.01). This finding suggests support for the hypothesis that the low number of unidirectional scar surface patterns among whole flakes may reflect preferential selection for larger tools knapped earlier in local core reduction sequences. These observations support the hypothesis of local tool production.

Superficially, the data on striking platform morphology do not seem to match the predictions of predominantly local tool production (Table 4.4). The more extensively-modified forms of striking platforms (facetted and dihedral) are more common than the less-modified forms. However, much of this pattern reflects a significantly disproportionate amount of facetted platforms found among smaller flakes, and fewer-than expected proportions of cortical and plain platforms among larger flakes (chi-square = 27.67, df =6, p <.01). Flakes with facetted platforms appear to be "swamping" all other aspects of striking platform variation.

The ratio between striking platform width and striking platform thickness, in principle, ought to reflect differences between the reduction of local raw materials and the reduction of raw materials brought from far away. The thickness of a striking platform is a mechanical constant: that is, a certain thickness is necessary to initiate fracture at a point far enough from the core edge to create flakes of useful size (Pelcin 1997). Conversely, any but the minimum amount of striking platform width is waste. That is, wider platforms consume part of the core surface that could otherwise be used to detach other flakes. It follows that in situations where raw material is scarce, as would be the case if it was transported from afar, there should have been strong incentives to conserve (i.e., to minimize striking platform width relative to thickness). In situations where raw materials were procured locally, there should have been few such incentives to conserve, and one ought not to expect significant difference in the ration of striking platform width/striking platform thickness among flakes of differing sizes.

This model was tested with data on the technological length and striking platform width/thickness ratios on whole flakes from Ar Rasfa (n = 972)(see Table 4.5). Congruent with the predictions of a local procurement model, there is no relationship between smaller flake sizes and relatively narrower striking platforms (r² = .01, p <.01).

There are other, less precisely quantifiable reasons to rule out a significant exotic source for the Ar Rasfa assemblage. Most of the flakes are relatively large and unretouched. Such retouched tools as are present in the assemblage are minimally modified, and there are few of the heavily-retouched tools (convergent scrapers, bifaces, cores on flakes) that are common in assemblages from Middle Paleolithic sites where local raw materials are scarce (Rolland and Dibble 1990).

In terms of all the variables considered here, including

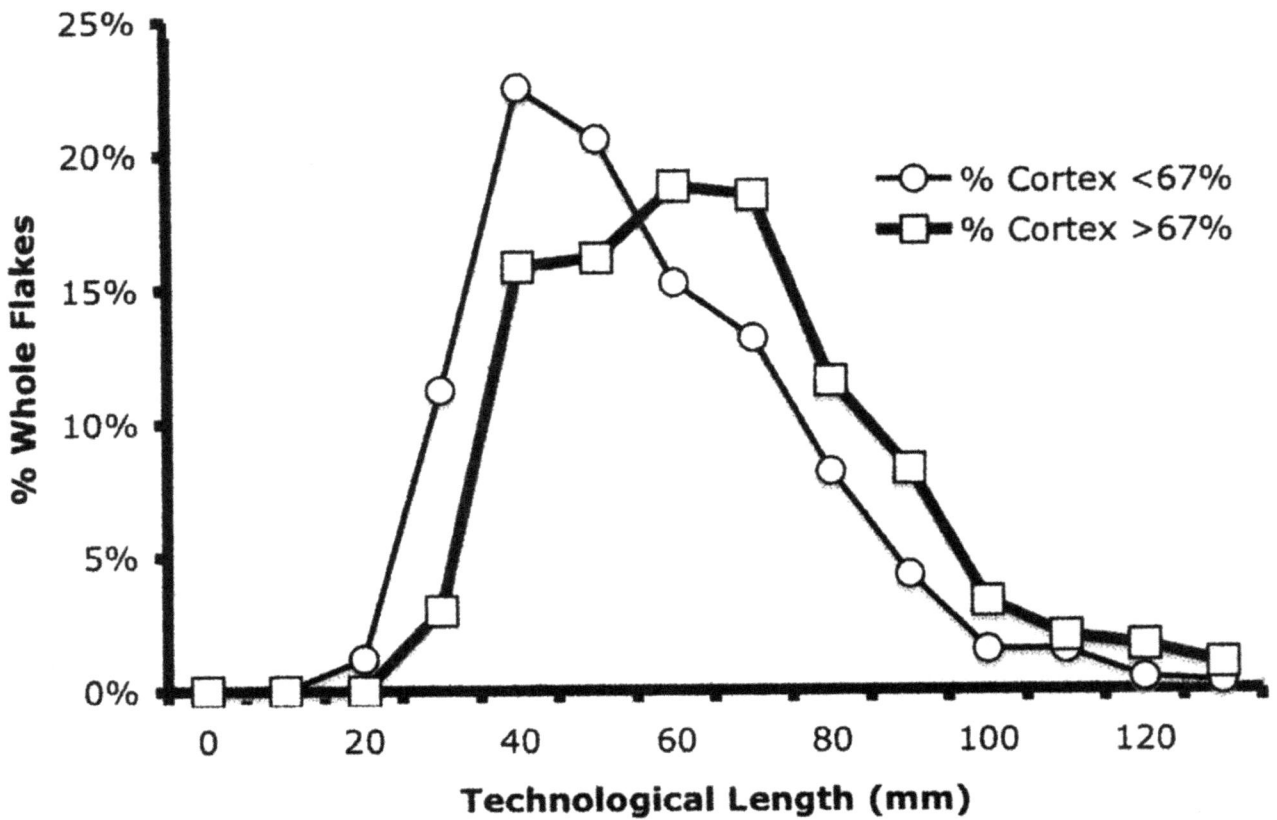

Figure 4.1 Graph showing cortex extent vs. flake technological length.

Table 4.1 Cortex extent (simplified) on flakes of varying length in the Ar Rasfa assemblage.

Flake Technological Length (mm)	Cortex <67%		Cortex >67%	
	n	%	n	%
0	0	0	0	0
10	0	0	0	0
20	8	1	0	0
30	76	11	9	3
40	152	22	48	16
50	139	21	49	16
60	103	15	57	19
70	89	13	56	18
80	55	8	35	12
90	29	4	25	8
100	10	1	10	3
110	10	1	6	2
120	3	0	5	2
>120	2	0	3	1
Total	676	100	303	100

Table 4.2 Dorsal surface morphology vs. technological length for whole flakes.

Dorsal Surface Morphology	< 50 mm	51-100 mm	>100 mm	n	%
1. All Cortical	67	56	1	124	13
2. Partly Cortical -Distal	45	44	3	92	9
3. Partly Cortical -Right	54	76	3	133	14
4. Partly Cortical -Left	58	65	9	132	13
(1-4. Subtotal Cortical)	(224)	(241)	(16)	(481)	(49)
5. Relict Edge -Distal	2	5		7	1
6. Relict Edge -Right	13	9		22	2
7. Relict Edge -Left	7	5		12	1
(5-7. Subtotal Relict Edge)	(22)	(19)		(41)	(4)
8. Unidirectional-parallel	77	59	1	137	14
9. Unidirectional-convergent	22	28	3	53	5
(8-9. Subtotal Unidirectional)	(99)	(87)	(4)	(190)	(19)
10. Radial/Centripetal	45	35	1	81	8
11. Bidirectional-Opposed	47	67	8	122	12
(10-11. Subtotal Multidirectional)	(92)	(102)	(9)	(203)	(21)
12. Other	5	2		7	1
13. Indeterminate	43	18		61	6
Total	485	469	29	983	100
%	49	48	3	100	10

Table 4.3. Frequencies of dorsal surface morphology (simplified) for retouched tools.

Dorsal Surf Morphology	n	%
1-4. Cortical Subtotal	32	34
5-7. Subtotal Relict Edge	4	4
8-9. Unidirectional Subtotal	17	18
10-11. Multidirectional Subtotal	23	24
12. Other	2	2
13. Indeterminate	17	18
Total	95	100

Table 4.4. Striking platform morphology vs. flake length.

Striking Platform Morphology	0-50mm	51-100mm	>100mm	n	%
Cortical	27	22		49	6
Plain	99	84	2	185	23
Dihedral	19	8		27	3
Facetted	313	460	29	802	100
Total	458	574	31	1063	
%	43	54	3	100	

Table 4.5 Width/thickness ratio values for flakes of varying length.

Statistic	0-50mm	51-100mm	>100mm	n
Mean	3.58	3.30	2.63	3.39
Standard Deviation	2.07	1.71	1.10	1.90
Count	396	544	32	972
%	41	56	3	100

59

Table 4.6. Technological artifact types and core reduction stages. Parentheses enclose subtotals.

Technological Type	Activity	Total	%	% Identifiable Subtotals (n/1418)
Naturally-backed flake	Core-Preparation	7	0.4	
Whole cortical flake	Core-Preparation	481	28.2	
	(Core Preparation)	(488)	(28.6)	34.4
Levallois point	Core-Exploitation	61	3.6	
Levallois blade	Core-Exploitation	34	2	
Levallois flake	Core-Exploitation	179	10.5	
Whole non-cortical flake	Core-Exploitation	189	11.1	
	(Core-Exploitation)	(463)	(27.2)	32.7
Core-trimming flake	Core-Rejuvenation	80	4.7	6
	(Core-Rejuvenation)	(80)	(4.7)	
Cores	Discard	279	16.4	
Retouched tool	Discard	108	6.3	
	(Discard)	(387)	(22.7)	27.3
	Identifiable Subtotal	(1418)	(83.2)	100.0
Flake fragment-non-proximal	Indeterminate	198	11.6	
Flake fragment-proximal	Indeterminate	79	4.6	
Blocky fragment	Indeterminate	10	0.6	
Total		1705	100	

cortex extent, dorsal surface morphology, striking platform morphology, and striking platform width/thickness ratio, the Ar Rasfa assemblage exhibits technological characteristics suggesting local raw material procurement.

This conclusion would be stronger if it were supported by raw material source tracing data. Such research is an obvious subject for future fieldwork, but it cannot be carried out at present without extensive geological reconnaissance, source surveys, and geophysical analysis of both well-provenienced rocks samples and archaeological specimens. At present, based on visual inspection, there do not appear to be any flint/chert samples in the Ar Rasfa assemblage that differ from those available locally.

Tool Manufacturing Strategies

Geneste (1985), working in France, has introduced a framework for describing the major aspects of Middle Paleolithic tool production. He did this by relating individual technical operations, segments of the larger operational sequence (*chaîne opératoire*) to specific groups of technologically-defined flake types. There are four groups of these technical activities: core preparation, core exploitation, core rejuvenation and tool repair/discard.

The artifact types that most clearly reflect core preparation are cortical flakes. The artifact types that most clearly reflect core exploitation are Levallois flakes and other non-cortical flakes. Core-trimming elements (essentially any tool with a relict edge on it more extensive than the

immediate area of the point of percussion) and the cores themselves reflect core rejuvenation. Retouched tools and fragments of retouched tools reflect tool repair and discard. One can assess the relative significance of these activities for assemblage formation by converting the technological tool types tabulated in Chapter 3 into one or another of these activity categories (see Table 4.6).

Of the 1705 artifacts from Ar Rasfa, 1418 (83.2%) can be assigned to a particular knapping activity. The remainder, mostly flake fragments and blocky fragments cannot be assigned to a particular activity and are considered "indeterminate".

Among the identifiable artifacts, about even proportions are referable to core preparation and core exploitation (34 and 33%, respectively, or 67% collectively). The next most common implied activity reflects discard behavior (27%). In this category, cores outnumber retouched tools by a ratio of more than two to one. This disproportion of cores vs. retouched tools reinforces the picture of flintknapping at the site as primarily focused on core reduction rather than on tool repair. Core preparation accounts for 13.8% of the artifacts. There is a ratio of approximately five exploitation flakes for each cortical flake and a ratio of 2.7 core exploitation flakes for each core. Curiously, there is only one core rejuvenation flake for every 3.5 cores, suggesting core recycling/rejuvenation was not a common activity. This is exactly consistent with reduction of local raw materials, a situation in which there are few incentives to conserve raw material.

Artifact Refitting

There are several other avenues to reconstructing tool manufacturing strategies at Ar Rasfa. Refitting analysis is one such avenue. The 1997 collections were brought to Stony Brook University for study and a search was conducted for refitting/conjoining flakes. Conjoins are flakes that were once whole but have been broken (e.g., distal and proximal fragments of the same flake). Refits or refitting sets are groups of flakes and/or cores that are divided by conchoidal fractures (e.g., flakes struck one after the other from the same flake-release surface)(Cziesla 1990).

One refitting set comprised of two flakes and a core (#1.102, 1.52, and 1.181) was discovered among the artifacts from Test Pit 1 (Figure 4.2). Artifact #1.102 is a hinge-terminated non-cortical flake. Artifact #1.52 is a large partly-cortical flake that was struck from a much larger core with unidirectional-parallel surface preparation. Artifact #1.102 refits to a concavity immediately adjacent to the striking platform on the dorsal surface of #1.52. It seems to reflect a failed attempt to detach a larger flake. It seems as though Artifact #1.102 was detached next, but with so much force and so little skill that it vastly overshot the flake-release surface, removing a significant amount of the distal end of the core. Artifact #1.181 is a core fragment with a worked edge prepared at one end and a flake-release surface that refits to the ventral face of #1.102. The striking platform preparation on #1.181 appears to have been an attempt (abandoned, as it turned out) to rejuvenate the core's flake-release surface after the detachment of #1.52.

It is perhaps telling that this one refitting set from the Ar Rasfa site records two flake detachments, both of which preserve evidence for the kind of flintknapping errors that are common among beginner flintknappers. There are not many obvious other knapping errors among the Ar Rasfa assemblage, and thus no reason to see the properties of this refitting set as statistically representative of the assemblage as a whole. Rather, it would have made sense for individuals learning how to knap stone, presumably children, to have practiced their skills at or near places where raw materials were locally abundant (Shea 2006a). Again, this observation reinforces the hypothesis that Ar Rasfa was a place where considerable knapping effort focused on the reduction of local raw materials.

Spatial patterning of microdébitage can also reveal significant information about horizontal variation in flintknapping activities, and thus potentially about tool production at Ar Rasfa. However, the limited spatial extent of the Ar Rasfa trenches precludes drawing any such study. If there were to be further research at the site, it might be possible to identify flintknapping areas like those found at Tor Faraj, Jordan, from concentrations of flake fragments and microdébitage (Henry 2003).

Tool Use Strategies

In discussing tool use, it is important to distinguish between modes of use (i.e., specific task such as butchery, woodworking, hide-preparation, etc.) and tool use strategies (i.e., different ways of accomplishing the same task). For example, in rural parts of Southwest Asia and North Africa, on the Eid al-Adha, the senior male of a traditional Muslim family butchers a sheep or a goat (Ahmad, personal experience). When they do so, most men perform the butchery with kitchen knives or other general-purpose knives. In a sense, this is an opportunistic strategy of tool use, the tool in question being selected from such implements as are immediately available; after use, the tool is again used for other purposes. In contrast, a professional urban butcher typically has expensive specialized butchery knives and other gear used solely for butchering sheep, goats and other animals. These more specialized tools are curated (transported from workshop to workshop by the individual butcher), and they are carefully maintained in good working order at all times.

The kinds of tasks performed with Levantine Middle Paleolithic tools are known mainly from the results of microwear analysis (Shea 1988, 1989a, 1989b, 1991, 1995b, 2007b). Among large, probabilistically-sampled assemblages from Kebara, Qafzeh, Tabun, Hayonim, and Tor Faraj, there do not appear to be any persistent patterns of form-function correlation. Rather, a wide range of formal tool types, both retouched tools and unmodified débitage were used for woodworking, butchery, and hide-working. One notable exception appears to be points/triangular flakes. These tools exhibit a disproportionate incidence of wear referable to spear point use, haft contact, and butchery (Shea 1988).

The strategies Levantine Middle Paleolithic humans used to accomplish these activities can be discussed in terms of either expedient or curated strategies (Binford 1979). In expedient strategies, tools are used opportunistically, more or less in the same frequency in which they occur on the surface of the ground in the immediate area where tool use is taking place. Data from microwear analyses of Levantine Middle Paleolithic assemblages (at least those that were probabilistically sampled) show precisely this proportionate relationship, except for Levallois points. These points seem to have been used and modified out of proportion to their relative abundance in Levantine Middle Paleolithic assemblages. This suggests that either these points were being used in tasks with high rates of edge-attrition and breakage, or that there was some other reason (perhaps even a symbolic/cultural one) why they were preferentially selected for use. These hypothesis are not mutually exclusive.

In the case of tools that are curated between episodes of use, one might reasonably expect efforts to make the tools conform to handles, to maximize potential utility (relatively high ratios of flake area to flake thickness). Such a strategy would result in overall greater evidence for retouch.

In order to test the expedient tool use model, retouched and unretouched tool counts were tabulated for broad technological artifact categories (noncortical whole flakes,

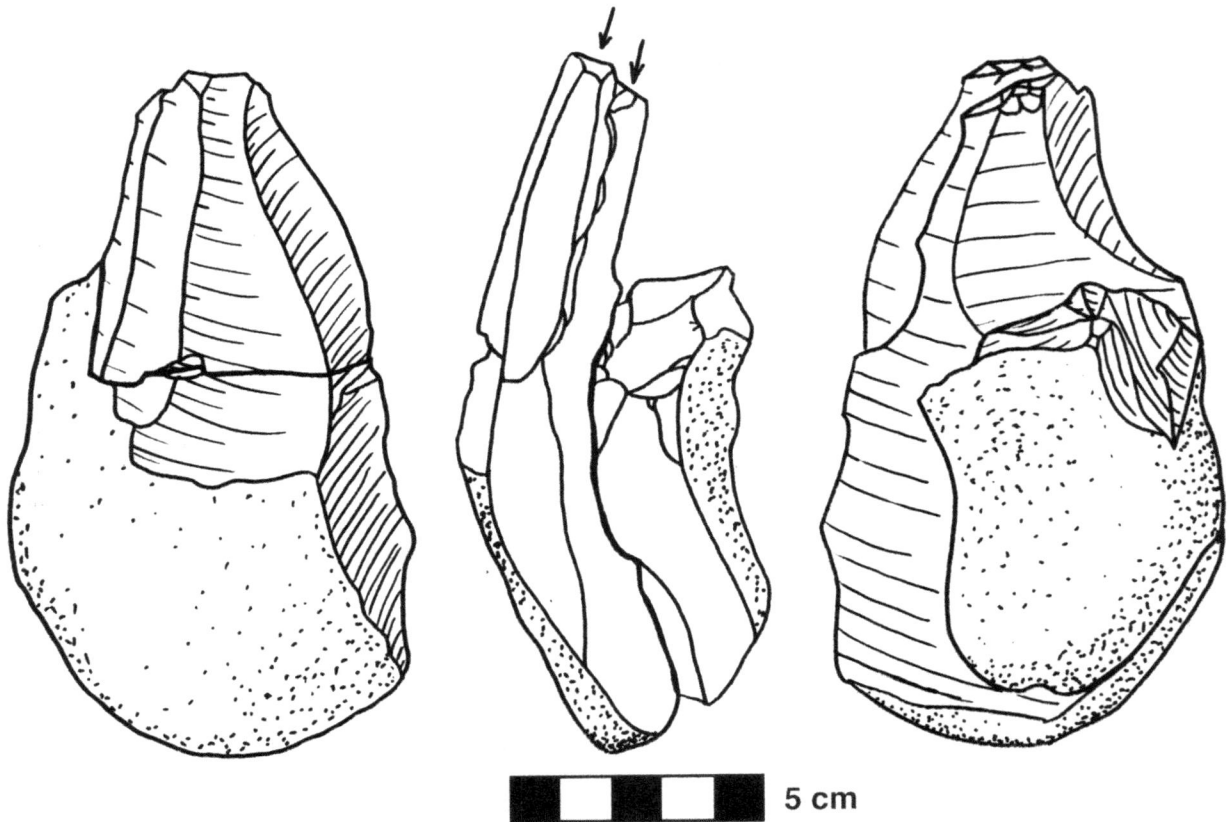

Figure 4.2 A refitting set of artifacts from Ar Rasfa Test Pit 1, Level 3 (for discussion, see text).

Table 4.7 Retouch vs. technological artifact categories.

Technological artifact categories	Retouched	Unretouched	n
Whole flakes	43	413	456
Cortical flakes	34	544	578
Proximal flake fragments	19	105	124
Other flake fragments	28	216	244
Other	5	19	24
Total	129	1297	1426
%	9	91	100

cortical whole flakes, proximal flake fragments, other flake fragments, and miscellaneous/other débitage)(Table 4.7). Superficially, the results seem to conform to the expedient tool use model. Retouched tools are rare overall (129/1426 = 9 % of all débitage) and particular technological artifact types appear to have been selected for use and/or retouch in much greater proportions than their occurrence in the assemblage. However, a closer examination and a chi-square test reveal a pattern wherein cortical flakes and proximal flake fragments (and thus relatively larger, thicker pieces) were retouched significantly more frequently than their proportionate representation in the assemblage (chi-square = 18.85, df = 4, p <.01). This finding suggests that tool use strategies at Ar Rasfa approximated an expedient pattern, but with significant residual variability not explicable in terms of expedient tool use.

It would be desirable for future research at Ar Rasfa to attempt microwear and/or residue analysis. These kinds of analyses were not possible in conjunction with the 1997 and 1999 excavations, owing to mechanical damage incurred by the tools in the course of excavation and transportation from the field.

Flake Width/Thickness Ratios and the Jelinek Index

Levantine Paleolithic archaeologists have long held that the mean and variance statistics of Width/thickness ratios of whole flakes provide a valid chronological estimate for later Lower and Middle Paleolithic assemblages (Jelinek 1982b). This belief is founded on a demonstration that both mean width/thickness ratio values and variance of width/thickness ratios increased through the long sequence of Paleolithic assemblages at Tabun Cave (Jelinek 1977, 1981, 1982a, 1982b). Though the precise geochronological anchor-points Jelinek proposed for the Tabun sequence have been largely refuted, the "Jelinek Index" does appear to have some lasting value for sorting Levantine Middle Paleolithic assemblages into broadly "earlier" and "later" phases. By earlier, one means Early Middle Paleolithic, or >130 Kya. By later, one means assemblages dating to <130-45 Kya (combining Shea's Middle and Later Middle Paleolithic). Table 4.12 shows published data on Width/thickness values for Levantine Middle Paleolithic assemblages organized in terms of Early vs. Later Middle Paleolithic. (The table also presents data on these assemblages' affinities with different phases of Copeland's (1975) three-phase model of Levantine Mousterian industrial variability.)

Width/thickness ratio values for all 717 whole flakes from Ar Rasfa yield the following statistics: mean = 4.02, median = 3.82, variance = 2.85. These values have a highly-skewed distribution. Restricting the calculations of statistics to the 693 data points within two standard deviations of the mean yields somewhat different statistics: mean = 3.84, median = 3.71, variance = 1.96. As can be seen in Table 4.12, these width/thickness values are the lowest known for any Levantine Mousterian assemblage. The only lower values are those for an unusually spatially restricted sample of stone tools from one excavation square of Amud Cave and a highly-selectively-curated sample from Skhul. The width/thickness ratio values of the Ar Rasfa sample are closest to those for Early Middle Paleolithic assemblages, such as those from Abu Sif, Tabun IX, Rosh Ein Mor, WHS 634/'Ain Difla, and Nahal Aqev 3. In terms of the Width/thickness index, the Ar Rasfa assemblage is more similar to Lower Paleolithic/Early Acheulean or early Middle Paleolithic assemblages than to later Middle Paleolithic assemblages.

Efficiency of Tool Production

The "Jelinek Index" is a longstanding measurement-based approach to characterizing Levantine Middle Paleolithic variability. Though it is clearly a methodological advance over subjective characterizations, its main weakness is that nobody knows what, in terms of hominin behavior, it is actually monitoring. It might, as Jelinek originally argued, reflect behavioral variability and flexibility, but there is no explicit body of middle-range theory that justifies this interpretation. A relatively new and promising way of examining lithic variability involves a "strategic perspective": one which measures the efficiency of tool production by relating the costs of flake production to the "benefits" it yields (Shea et al. 2007).

The "benefit" accrued from different flake production strategies can be measured by increased rates of cutting edge recovery. Leroi-Gourhan (1943) made one of the first efforts to do this explicitly by measuring ratios of cutting edge per unit mass of stone, but recent experimental studies have called into question the value of this approach. For example, simply measuring cutting edge/mass ratios on "finished" tools (as Leroi-Gourhan apparently did)

overlooks the unutilized waste created in the course of knapping them. Moreover, Leroi-Gourhan's frequently-cited conclusion that prismatic blades are widely believed to recover more cutting edge per unit mass of stone than other flakes is problematic, as in fact, they do not. Rather, it is simply that small blades, by virtue of their size recover more cutting edge. Triangular and sub-triangular products of discoidal core reduction, for example, recover just as much cutting edge per unit mass of stone as do blades (Eren et al. 2008).

Rather than viewing lithic production efficiency through a typological filter, with all the other potentially erroneous assumptions this involves, a better approach involves measuring production efficiency directly in term of metric variables (Shea et al. 2007). A flake with large surface area (technological length × width at midpoint of length) relative to thickness provides more potential cutting edge than flakes with smaller surface area values and/or greater thickness values. Among hard-hammer percussion byproducts, the "cost" of efficient flake production can be measured in terms of the width of the flake's striking platform relative to its thickness (Davis 2000, Davis and Shea 1998, Dibble 1997, Pelcin 1997). The principal morphological variable that controls the thickness of a flake is the distance between the point of fracture initiation and the external surface of a core: in other words, the thickness of a flake's striking platform. Flakes with minimal, narrow striking platforms leave in place portions of the worked edge that could be used as striking platforms for additional flakes. Flakes with relatively broad striking platforms remove portions of the core's working edge that could have been used as striking platforms for additional flake removals. As Shea and colleagues (2007: 160) phrased it,

[T]hese cost and benefit proxy measurements [can] be calculated from measurements archaeologists routinely make on flakes from African and Eurasian Paleolithic contexts. The two measurements involved are the flake surface area/flake thickness ratio (FSA/Th) and the striking platform width/striking platform thickness ratio (PW/PTh) measured on whole, unretouched flakes longer than 30mm. Assemblages that exhibit higher mean values of FSA/Th and lower values of PW/PTh reflect more efficient flake production than ones with lower mean values for FSA/Th and higher values for PW/PTh.

FSA/Th and PW/PTh ratios were calculated for all whole flakes with technological length values greater than 30mm. The statistical variation of these ratios is summarized in Table 4.8. Both FSA/Th and PW/PTh have unimodal but right-skewed distributions (i.e., a few specimens with large values), but their means (233.0 and 3.3, respectively) accurately reflect their central tendencies (Figures 4.3 and 4.4).

FSA/Th and PW/PTh values vary among the different tool categories in the Ar Rasfa assemblage. A bivariate plot of the mean FSA/Th and PW/PTh values for major morphological tool types shows an interesting division

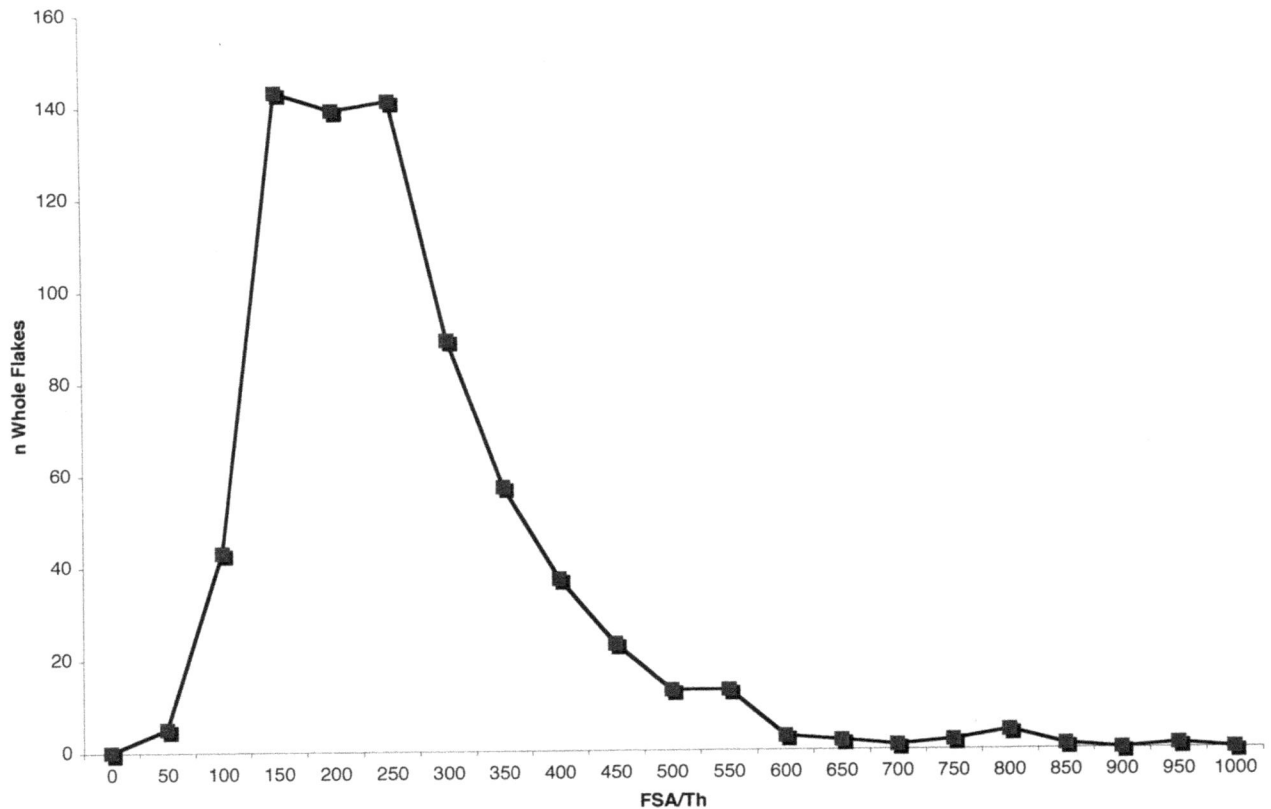

Figure 4.3 Histogram of FSA/Th values for whole flakes from Ar Rasfa.

(Figure 4.5). Levallois flakes, Levallois points, and naturally-backed flakes show high values of FSA/Th and PW/PTh. This indicates that they are recovering much potential utility, but at a correspondingly elevated cost. In a sense, their production involves a kind of technological intensification (expending more energy/cost to recover greater potential benefit/utility). Much of the increased "cost" associated with the production of these tools reflects their relatively wide striking platforms. A second group of artifacts, including whole flakes, Levallois blades, and core-trimming flakes shows low FSA/Th and PW/PTh values. These tools recover relatively less potential utility per unit of cost, largely because they are thicker than the first group.

Because this is an experimental, exploratory analysis, it does not take into account other variables that are plausibly linked to energy expenditure/efficiency variation in flake production. Two potentially revealing variables are cortex coverage and platform facetting.

In the initial stages of core reduction, there are few incentives to conserve raw material, and thus one might reasonably expect lower FSA/Th and PW/PTh values for cortical flakes (which are detached early in core reduction) than for non-cortical flakes (which are detached later on). To test this assumption, and for the sake of simplicity, flakes were sorted into two groups, those with <34% dorsal cortex on the one hand, and those with >34% cortex on the other. FSA/Th values vary in the predicted way, with less-cortical

flakes exhibiting significantly higher values (t= -4.30, df = 369, p<.01)(see Table 4.9). PW/PTh ratios, in contrast vary in the opposite direction, with less-cortical flakes showing significantly higher values (t= -5.05, df= 677, p<.01).

Lithic analysts view striking platform morphology as reflecting lesser or greater amounts of effort in core preparation. Cortical and plain striking platforms indicate less effort, dihedral and facetted ones more effort. If this is true, then FSA/Th and PW/PTh values for flakes with cortical and plain striking platforms should be lower than for flakes with dihedral and facetted striking platforms. This prediction is borne out by the Ar Rasfa flake data (t=6.94, df = 398, p <.01; see also Table 4.10). Similarly, one ought to expect greater efforts to minimize platform width as core reduction progresses, and thus smaller values of PW/PTh on flakes with facetted and dihedral striking platforms. As was the case with dorsal cortex coverage, however, this prediction is not supported by the Ar Rasfa data. Flakes with facetted and dihedral striking platforms have larger PW/PTh values than flakes with plain or cortical striking platforms (t= 4.22, df = 338, p <.01).

Finally, FSA/Th and PW/PTh values can be used to make inter-assemblage comparisons. Unfortunately, only a small number of Levantine Paleolithic assemblages have been studied in the same way as outlined above and have had their mean FSA/Th and PW/PTh values published (see Table 4.12). These assemblages include one Lower

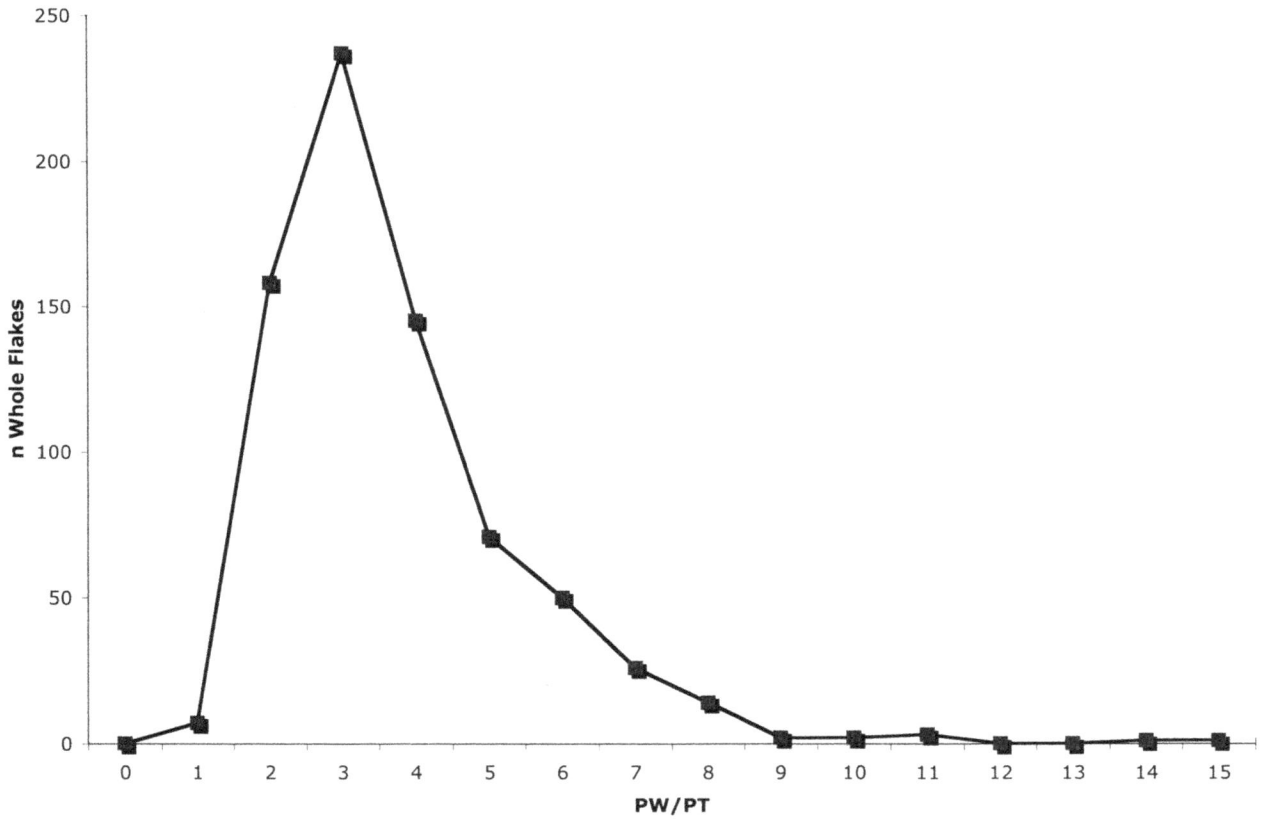

Figure 4.4 Histogram of PW/PTh values for whole flakes from Ar Rasfa.

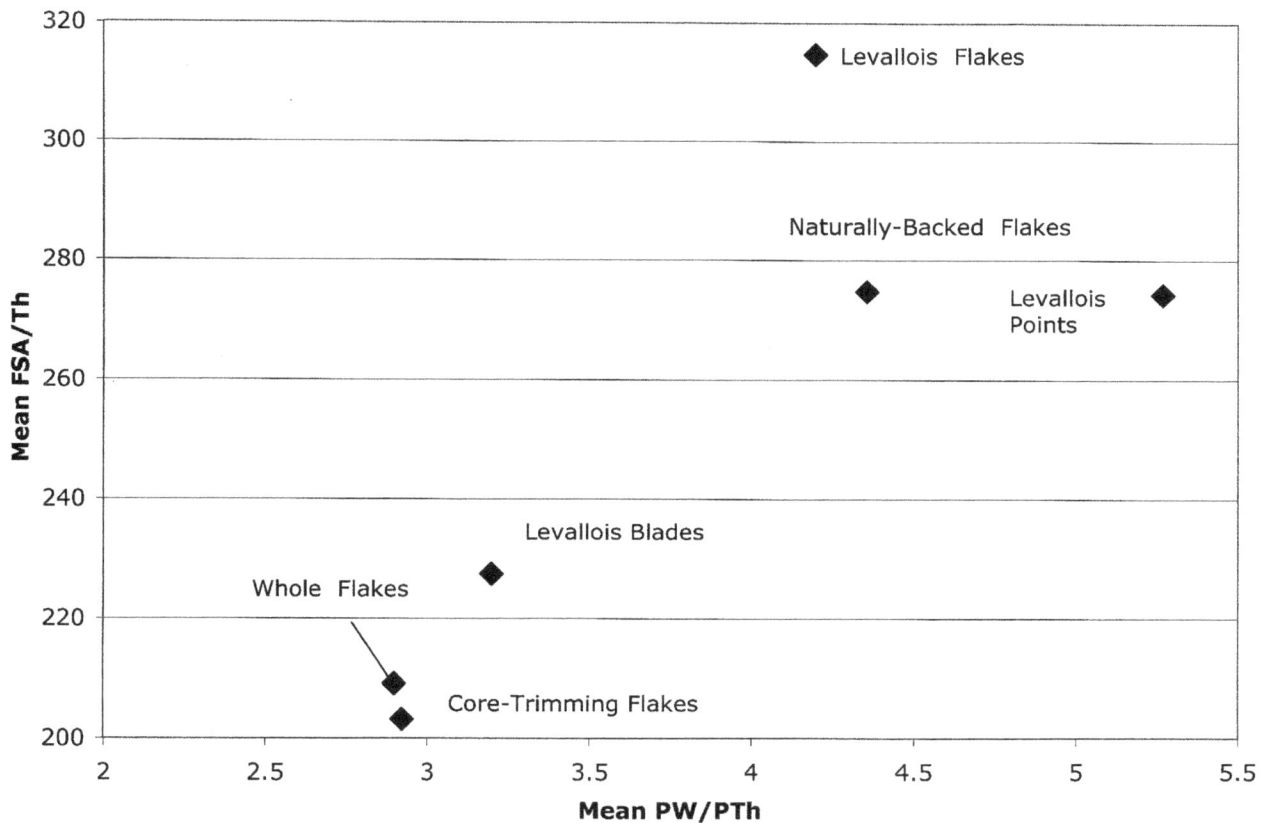

Figure 4.5 Scatterplot of mean FSA/Th and PW/PTh values for various technological tool types in the Ar Rasfa assemblage.

Table 4.9 Flake surface/area (FSA/Th) and striking platform width/thickness (PW/PTh) values for cortical and non-cortical flakes.

Cortex Coverage	Mean FSA/Th	SD	Mean PW/PT	SD	n	%
<34%	247.8	129.0	3.5	1.8	440	61
>34%	209.4	108.1	2.9	1.4	277	39
All Flakes	233.0	122.7	3.3	1.7	717	100

Table 4.10 Descriptive statistics for flake surface/area (FSA/Th) and striking platform width/thickness (PW/PTh).

Striking Platform Morphology	Mean FSA/Th	SD	Mean PW/PTh	SD	n	%
Facetted & dihedral	246.1	125.3	3.4	1.7	532	76
Plain & Cortical	185.6	88.7	2.9	1.4	169	24

Table 4.11. Width/thickness ratios for Levantine Middle Paleolithic assemblages.

Early vs. Later Middle Paleolithic	Complete Flakes	Mean	Median	Variance	n	Source
	Ar Rasfa (<7.5)	3.84	3.71	1.96	693	1
	Ar Rasfa (all)	4.02	3.82	2.85	717	1
Early	Abu Sif C	4.126	3.875	1.732	173	2
Early	Tabun IX	4.248	3.999	3.128	743	2
Early	Rosh Ein Mor	4.436	4.111	4.236	373	2
Early	Abu Sif B	4.510	4.002	3.342	214	2
Early	WHS 634/'Ain Difla	4.565	4.239	3.244	445	3
Early	Nahal Aqev 3	4.925	4.716	3.902	332	2
Early/Late	Skhul B2	6.532	5.833	11.405	113	2
Early/Late	Skhul B1	6.705	6.167	8.262	355	2
Late	Qafzeh L (Units XVII-XIX)	7.034	6.502	9.508	573	2
Late	Far'ah II	4.280	3.99	3.53	337	4
Late	Tabun I	4.633	4.249	5.049	1377	2
Late	Shukbah D	5.63	5.204	6.302	484	2
Late	Qafzeh I (Unit VIII)	6.476	5.802	7.974	661	2
Late	Amud B4	3.877			277	5
Late	Keoue III	4.419	4	3.637	295	5
Late	Keoue I	4.476	4.2	3.8674	128	5
Late	Amud B2	4.889			751	6
Late	Keoue II	5.048	4.4	8.5357	45	5
Late	El Wad G	5.616	5.123	5.694	213	2
Late	Kebara F (Unit 3)	5.891	5.332	7.129	604	2
Late	Kebara F (Unit 35)	5.962	5.496	7.604	628	2
Late	Kebara F (Unit 38)	6.293	5.668	8.166	539	2

1. This study, 2. Jelinek (1982a: 89-99), 3. Lindly and Clark (1987: 287), 4. Gilead and Grigson (1984: 76), 5.Calculated from Nishiaki and Copeland (1992), 6. Ohnuma (1992: 96).

Paleolithic (Early Acheulean) sample ('Ubeidiya Unit III-20/22), several Middle Paleolithic assemblages (Rosh Ein Mor [two samples], SMU D40), and four Upper Paleolithic assemblages (Boker (SMU D100a), SMU D31 Upper, Ein Aqev East (SMU D34), and SMU D31 Lower). The mean FSA/Th and PW/PTh values of whole flakes from these assemblages are plotted together with those for Ar Rasfa in Figure 4.6. As shown in this chart, the mean FSA/Th and PW/PTh values for Ar Rasfa differ from those of other Levantine Middle Paleolithic assemblages in the direction of more efficient flake production (i.e., higher "benefit", lower "cost"). In fact, these are essentially identical to those for the Levantine Upper Paleolithic assemblage from Boker (SMU D100a). This being said, the Ar Rasfa FSA/Th and PW/PTh values are not markedly different from the range of values for other Middle Paleolithic and Middle Stone Age assemblages. The larger lesson one can infer from these data is that the efficiency of flake production cuts across traditional typological and chronostratigraphic divisions of the Paleolithic archaeological record. It follows that

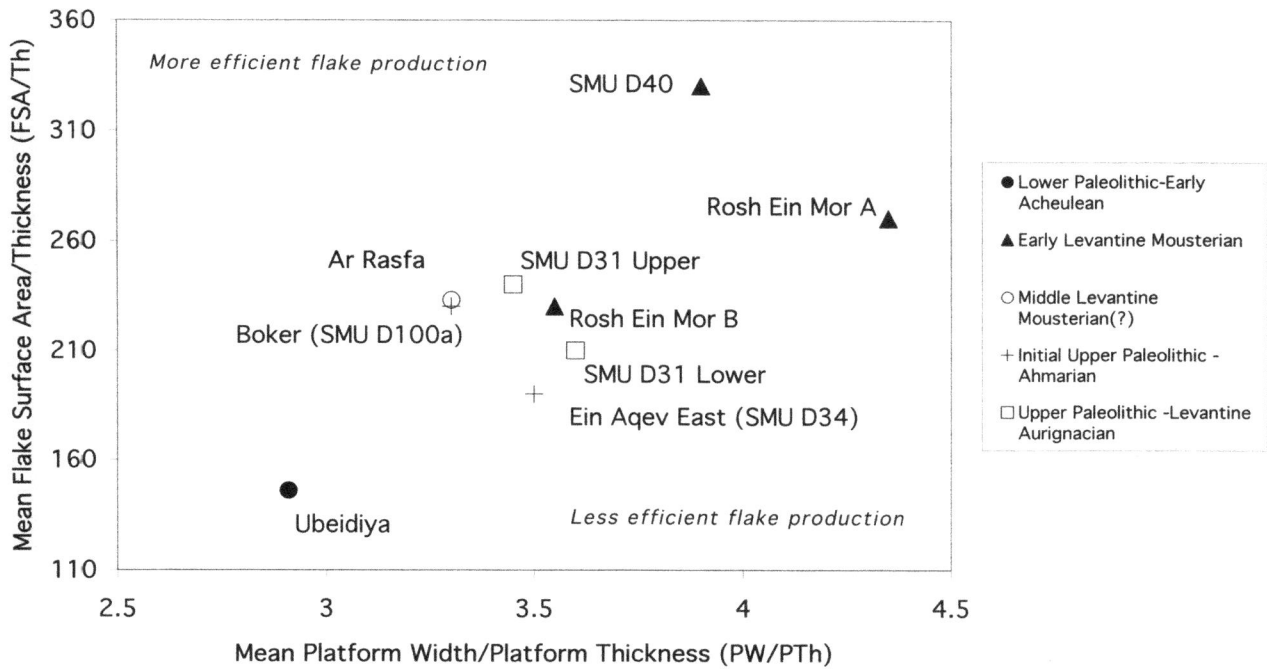

Figure 4.6 Scatterplot of mean FSA/Th and PW/PTh values for selected Levantine Lower, Middle, and Upper Paleolithic assemblages.

Table 4.12 Flake surface/area (FSA/Th) and striking platform width/thickness (PW/PTh) values for selected Levantine Paleolithic assemblages.

Assemblage	Industry	PW/PT	FSAT	n	Source
'Ubeidiya III-20/22	Lower Paleolithic-Early Acheulean	2.91	146	182	1
Rosh Ein Mor A (SMU D15)	Early Levantine Mousterian	4.35	270	213	2
Rosh Ein Mor C (SMU D15)	Early Levantine Mousterian	3.55	230	200	2
SMU D40	Early Levantine Mousterian	3.9	330	157	2
Ar Rasfa	Middle Levantine Mousterian (?)	3.30	233.00	717	3
Boker (SMU D100a)	Upper Paleolithic-Ahmarian	3.3	230	133	2
Ein Aqev East (SMU D34)	Upper Paleolithic-Ahmarian	3.5	190	107	2
SMU D31 lower	Upper Paleolithic-Levantine Aurignacian	3.6	210	128	2
SMU D31 upper	Upper Paleolithic-Levantine Aurignacian	3.45	240	83	2

NOTES: Sources: 1. Shea and Bar Yosef (1999), 2. Dibble (1997), 3. This study.

viewing technological differences among chronologically-sequential Paleolithic assemblages as simple reflections of increased technological efficiency is probably a mistake. Needless to say, this preliminary impression of these data needs to be tested with additional measurements of flake production efficiency from many other regions and time periods.

CHAPTER 5.

CONCLUSION

Our limited understanding of the age of Ar Rasfa precludes detailed reconstruction of the ways in which the site was integrated into Middle Paleolithic human land-use strategies. However, whether the site was occupied during warm humid conditions like those present today or during colder and drier phases, the position of the Ar Rasfa site on a rich flint source and near the Jordan River/Lisan paleo-lake would have made it an attractive place for human settlement (See Figure 5.1). Both today, and in the past, the site is located in a steppic ecotone between the riverine habitats of the Jordan Valley and the woodlands of the Transjordan Plateau. The traces of toolmaking that we find at Ar Rasfa plausibly reflect prehistoric humans "gearing up" (preparing replacements for components of mobile toolkits) for foraging forays to higher elevations as well as provisioning themselves with tools for local use.

Overview of Findings

The stone tools recovered from Ar Rasfa were analyzed using a technological and typological framework described in Chapter 2. This framework employed both traditional approaches to characterizing stone tool technology as well as methodologically innovative analytical approaches to the study of retouched edges and flake production efficiency. Separate analyses were carried out on cores, flakes, retouched tools and retouched tool edges. These analyses examined variation in artifact relative frequencies as well as variation in key morphological attributes and metric variables. The principal findings of this analysis are summarized below.

Typological Characteristics of the Ar Rasfa Assemblage

Levallois cores are the most common type of core in the Ar Rasfa assemblage. Most of these Levallois cores feature bidirectional-opposed and radial centripetal surface preparation, a pattern that contrasts with flake dorsal surface preparation, among which the most common patterns are unidirectional-parallel and bidirectional-convergent (among non-cortical flakes and non-core-trimming elements). Other core types that are present include cores-on-flakes

and choppers. Once thought to be rare, cores-on-flakes are recognized as a common feature of Levantine Mousterian assemblages. Levantine prehistorians also also describe them as "Nahr Ibrahim cores" and "Jerf Ajla cores" (Hovers 2007). Choppers are traditionally thought to be rare in Middle Paleolithic assemblages, but they are found at Ar Rasfa in relatively high proportions. Unlike Lower Paleolithic choppers, whose battered edges suggest use, the choppers from Ar Rasfa may not be purposefully shaped artifacts, but rather pebble-cores that were tested for suitability, rejected and discarded on the spot. As is often the case in Levantine Mousterian assemblages, a small number of "prismatic" cores (i.e., blade cores) were found as well.

Among débitage/detached pieces, the most common kinds of artifacts are whole non-Levallois flakes, Levallois flakes and flake fragments. The least common débitage types are naturally-backed flakes and block fragments.

The high percentage of Levallois flakes and cores in the Ar Rasfa assemblage, paired with the relatively small number of retouched tools, are characteristics shared by most Levantine Mousterian assemblages. Among Levallois débitage, flakes vastly outnumber blades and points.

Cortex is relatively common on flake dorsal surfaces (about 50% of all débitage), but flakes with more than 67% dorsal cortex only amount to 9.5% of the Ar Rasfa débitage. Facetted, dihedral and plain striking platforms predominate in the assemblage. This suggests that while some initial core preparation took place at Ar Rasfa, most of the débitage resulted from core exploitation.

Dividing the total number of whole flakes and proximal flake fragments (n= 1219) by the number of cores (n=277) yields a flake:core ratio of 4.4 flakes per core in the assemblage. This figure is much lower than the number of flake scars longer than 30mm on most cores, suggesting that the Ar Rasfa assemblage is missing a significant number of flakes knapped on site. Taken at face value, these observations could suggest that local Middle Paleolithic

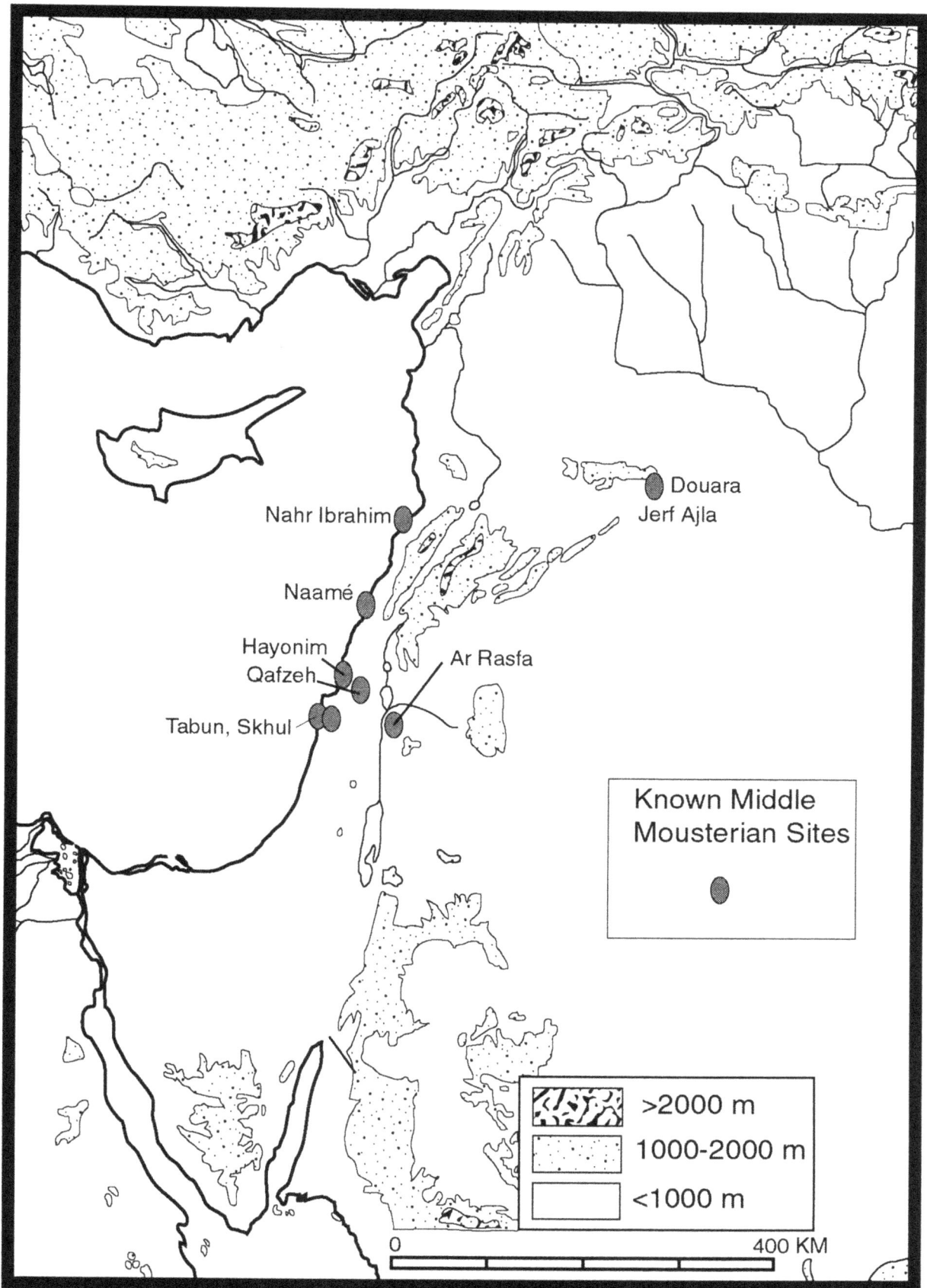

Figure 5.1 Map of Levant showing known locations¬ of Middle Mousterian assemblages (modified from Shea 2008, used with permission).

humans treated Ar Rasfa as a source from which they procured whole flakes for use elsewhere. Alternatively, this pattern may reflect sample error. As shown at Tor Faraj (Henry et al. 2004), Amud (Alperson-Afil and Hovers 2005), and Biqat Quneitra (Goren-Inbar 1990), flake to core ratios can vary widely across the surface of Levantine Middle Paleolithic sites. This issue can only be addressed by additional controlled excavations at Ar Rasfa.

There are only 95 retouched tools in the Ar Rasfa assemblage: the most common categories are truncations, notches, and various kinds of scrapers. If one lumps together the various scraper and scraper-like artifacts (truncations, transverse scrapers and sidescrapers, n = 42), such "scrapers" emerge as the most common retouched tool type. Retouched Levallois points, backed knives, and awls are conspicuously rare in the Ar Rasfa assemblage.

This study also presented statistical data on variation in retouched edge morphology. Most retouched edges were either concave or straight. On average, retouch extends 11 mm onto the (typically dorsal) surface of the tool. It is difficult to say much more than this because comparative measurement-based descriptions of retouched edges are rare in the published literature of Levantine Middle Paleolithic archaeology (Bisson 2000).

Assemblage Formation Processes: Procurement, Production, Use, and Discard.

This analysis has attempted to go beyond merely characterizing tool frequencies to shed light on Middle Paleolithic humans' technological strategies.

It is a common practice in prehistoric archaeology to refer to sites where stone tools were made as "quarry sites", but this name overlooks the fact that at many such sites there is evidence for tool discard and abandonment. Nor are these sites strictly analogous to modern day trash-disposal facilities, for they are demonstrably places were new tools were fashioned, both from raw materials and from artifacts made by previous site occupants. As Isaac (1981) proposed for Early Paleolithic sites in East Africa, it is probably most realistic to view lithic assemblages from any given locality as reflecting complex combinations of early human decisions about tool production, abandonment, and discard.

While raw material procurement interpretations are provisional, because no geophysical methods have yet been applied to raw material source identification, visual analysis indicates that raw material procurement at Ar Rasfa was primarily local. Most of the flint/chert in the assemblage appears to be of the same tan-grey Middle Cenomanian flint as is currently eroding from local bedrock and preserved in both nodular form and as clasts in gravel deposits near the site. The nearest non-Cenomanian flint, the black chert eroding from Lower Eocene deposits near the Yarmuk River and the Golan Heights, is not present in the Ar Rasfa assemblage.

No materials other than nodular or clastic flint/chert are present in the assemblage. In principle, local chert beds and siliceous limestone can be knapped, but the Middle Paleolithic knappers at Ar Rasfa appear to have bypassed these relatively inferior raw materials.

We have no information about the raw materials used as hammerstones by the Ar Rasfa knappers. It seems reasonable to assume they used local limestone. Inasmuch as modern-day knappers can use one hammerstone to detach thousands of flakes, the absence of hammerstones in the excavated assemblage probably reflects inadequate sampling.

In terms of tool manufacturing strategies, all stages of core reduction are represented: core preparation (cortical flakes), core exploitation (Levallois and non-Levallois flakes), core rejuvenation (flakes with relict edges/core-trimming elements), and discard/abandonment (cores themselves). Core preparation accounts for more than half of the débitage referable to one or another of these activities, while core exploitation and core rejuvenation account for smaller proportions. This finding is consistent with the hypothesis that Ar Rasfa was a site at which Middle Paleolithic humans replaced worn-out tools with freshly-knapped ones.

One innovative aspect of this study was a morphometric analysis of flake production efficiency using a strategic "cost/benefit" approach proposed by Shea and colleagues (Davis 1999, Davis and Shea 1998, Shea et al. 2007). For the Ar Rasfa flake assemblage, values of Flake Surface Area/Flake Thickness (FSA/Th -a proxy measurement for the potential utility or "benefit" derived from knapping) are relatively high. Indeed, they are close to FSA/Th values achieved by Levantine Upper Paleolithic humans knapping blades. Higher FSA/Th values are known for other Middle Paleolithic assemblages, however. The corresponding "cost" of the Ar Rasfa knappers' toolmaking strategies, measured by the ratio of Striking Platform Width/Striking Platform Thickness (SPW/SPTh), is also relatively low. Yet it is not as low as many Levantine Lower and Middle Paleolithic assemblages. In sum, the efficiency of flake production at Ar Rasfa entailed a relatively high ratio of benefit per unit of cost. However, it is possible that this analysis underestimates actual production efficiency, because flakes with greater potential utility are likely to have been taken away from the Ar Rasfa area for use in chert/flint-poor areas at higher elevations and elsewhere in the Jordan Valley. At present, there is no way to gauge the difference between actual flake production efficiency and that indicated by analysis of the stone tools remaining at Ar Rasfa.

The strongest evidence concerning artifact discard behavior at Ar Rasfa comes from retouched tools. Retouched edges are less sharp than freshly-knapped/unretouched tools, and thus the presence of retouched tools at Ar Rasfa may reflect early human decisions to abandon these tools and to replace them with unretouched artifacts of the same or greater size. A convex edge provides the maximum possible cutting edge, but as it is resharpened such edges tend to become concave (Dibble 1995). The predominance of concave and straight plan shapes among retouched edges from Ar Rasfa is consistent with the abandonment of heavily-utilized tools. Retouched tools are not particularly common at Ar Rasfa, and thus, in the balance, the lithic assemblage from the site is dominated by lithic by-products of tool production.

Comparisons to Other Assemblages

The technological and typological characteristics of the Ar Rasfa assemblage are not identical to any other known Levantine Middle Paleolithic assemblage. It is not completely alien from them, but there are complex points of similarity and difference. Putting the Ar Rasfa assemblage in culture-historical and ecological context can best be done by a series of ever-more-inclusive comparisons, first within Jordan itself, next within the Levant, and finally within Southwest Asia and the larger Middle Paleolithic "world".

Comparison to Jordanian Middle Paleolithic Assemblages

Numerous Middle Paleolithic sites have been identified in Jordan (see Figure 1.2), but only a small number of these have been subjected to controlled scientific excavations. These include sites at Tabaqat Fahl, Wadi el-Hasa, and Tor Faraj and Tor Sabiha.

At Tabaqat Fahl, near Pella, Macumber and colleagues (1992) surveyed and trenched a series of Late Pleistocene deposits ringing the lower end of the Wadi al-Hammeh. Their efforts did not result in the discovery of a large and discrete site like Ar Rasfa; rather, they found a constant low-density deposit of Middle Paleolithic artifacts. Like Ar Rasfa, these Mousterian occurrences are of an indeterminate age, though they are suspected to date to Late Pleistocene times on the basis of their position above the Abu Habil Gravel Formation. Though Tabaqat Fahl is only 10 km north of Ar Rasfa, this pattern of archaeological occurrences contrasts with that seen in the lower Wadi Yabis. It would be highly unusual for there to have been two completely different settlement patterns in the lower reaches of wadi systems so close to one another ecologically and geographically. It is also possible that this contrast is an artifact of preservation. Either large sites near Tabaqat Fahl have been lost to erosion, or the Ar Rasfa site may appear to be more discrete than it really is, owing to erosion and loss of sediments in the surrounding hills.

The Tabaqat Fahl assemblages have been only superficially described, and thus no detailed comparison with the Ar Rasfa assemblages is possible. Macumber and colleagues report one concentrated occurrence of Middle Paleolithic tools at sites WH 41, among which Levallois points and cores with unidirectional-convergent preparation are said to be common. These characteristics differ from the Ar Rasfa assemblage, among which Levallois points are rare and cores with radial-centripetal and bidirectional preparation predominate. In these respects, the Tabaqat Fahl assemblages seem to have more in common with Later Mousterian assemblages like those from Tor Faraj and Tor Sabiha in Jordan, or those from Kebara Cave in Israel and Shukhbah Cave in Palestine, all of which date to ca. 75-45 Kya.

In the Wadi el Hasa (western Jordan), Clark and colleagues (1997) excavated a Middle Paleolithic assemblage from the 'Ain Difla Rockshelter (WHS 634). The 'Ain Difla Rockshelter lies close to a fossil lake bed, now dissected by Wadi el Hasa. Mousterian artifacts and a sparse bone assemblage have been recovered from colluvial and alluvial deposits preserved against the back wall of the cave. ESR assays dated these Mousterian deposits to ca. 141 Kya.

The 'Ain Difla lithic assemblage is an Early Mousterian one, characterized by unidirectional-paralleled and bidirectional-opposed core surface preparation and by the production of elongated flakes, points, and blades. Retouched tools include ostensibly "Upper Paleolithic" forms such as burins and endscrapers, as well as distinctive "Abu Sif knives" (elongated Mousterian points and Levallois points). These characteristics contrast with the Ar Rasfa assemblage, in which endscrapers and burins are rare and Abu Sif knives are few in number. This being said, the deepest levels of Ar Rasfa preserved a small number of (largely unretouched) points, flakes, and blades immediately overlying the boulder conglomerate.

Two of the best-documented Middle Paleolithic sites in Jordan are Tor Faraj and Tor Sabiha, both located in the Himsa Basin, northeast of Aqaba. Both sites were discovered and excavated by Henry (1995b, 2003), though Tor Faraj has been the subject of more detailed analysis. Both sites are rockshelters located in sandstone cliffs at relatively high elevations (>1000 m). Henry assigned the lithic assemblages from Tor Faraj and Tor Sabiha to the Later Mousterian. They differ from each other mainly in ways thought referable to contrasting seasonal occupations. Assemblages from both sites share a similar raw material economy (mostly local low-quality materials). Technologically and typologically, however, both the Tor Faraj and Tor Sabiha assemblages differ from Ar Rasfa. At these sites the principal core preparation method involved unidirectional-convergent surface preparation and the systematic, in-bulk production of relatively short, wide-based Levallois points. As noted previously, at Ar Rasfa unidirectional-convergent surface preparation is rare (66/534 or 12.4% of flakes showing multiple dorsal scars), and Levallois points are uncommon.

One possible reason for the difference between Ar Rasfa and the Tor Faraj/Tor Sabiha assemblages may be the influence of environment and local food sources on Levallois point production. Both Shea (1995a) and Henry (1995a) have proposed that elevated levels of Levallois point production at these and other sites reflect variation in Middle Paleolithic human hunting strategies. In steppic areas, where large mammal prey populations migrate seasonally or follow predictable paths across the landscape, human hunters are under pressure to maximize energetic returns for hunting during narrow "windows of opportunity." Recent human hunter-gatherers cope with such constraints by making improvements to their weapons and other tools to increase reliability (i.e., "stopping power")(Bleed 1986). Attaching stone or metal points to projectiles and other hunting weapons is one such "reliability-enhancing" strategy (Shea 1997). Microwear and other contextual evidence (Boëda et al. 1999, Shea 1988) suggest Levallois points were used as weapon tips, though morphometric studies suggest they were more likely used as armatures for heavy, hand-cast spears or thrusting spears than as projectile points (Shea 2006c). Similar patterns of point-rich Middle Paleolithic assemblages are also known from the Zagros Mountains in Iraq and Iran (e.g., Shanidar, Bisitun, Warwasi and Kunji caves, see below)(Lindly 2005). Admittedly, Levallois-point-rich assemblages also occur at some lowland sites, such as Kebara and Amud, in contexts likely associated with dense woodland environments. This does not refute Shea's/Henry's hypotheses, however, it merely suggests that point production reflects multiple dimensions of hominin behavior.

Comparison to Levantine Middle Paleolithic Assemblages

Ar Rasfa joins a small number of excavated and well-documented Levantine Middle Paleolithic sites. Other such sites include Naamé, Tirat Carmel, Biqat Quneitra, Rosh Ein Mor, Nahal Aqev and sites sampled by deep sounding excavations around spring deposits at Umm el Tlel and El Kowm. Ar Rasfa shares with these open-air sites generally low frequencies of retouched tools, high frequencies of Levallois débitage, and relatively large cores and flakes. Of these open-air sites, Ar Rasfa's geological and geographic context is probably closest to Tirat Carmel, a site located on a flint-rich terrace on the Mediterranean side of Mount Carmel (Ronen 1974).

One other important way Ar Rasfa differs from most other Levantine Mousterian sites is that it is located at low elevation (37 meters below sea level). Only Amud Cave is located at a lower elevation. Ar Rasfa and similar sites in northwestern Jordan have the potential to shed light on the nature of Middle Paleolithic human activities on an ecological "frontier", the hyper-arid coastlines of the Rift Valley lakes.

It is not easy to assign the Ar Rasfa lithic assemblage to one or another of these Levantine Mousterian Phases. The Ar Rasfa assemblage differs most clearly from Early Levantine Mousterian assemblages. It lacks any significant laminar aspect, that is, blades are relatively uncommon. Endscrapers, burins, and elongated convergent scrapers/points are rare or absent.

However, the Ar Rasfa assemblage does not share the key defining features of Later Levantine Mousterian assemblages, such as predominantly unidirectional-convergent and radial-centripetal core preparation, or systematic Levallois point production.

Probably the closest parallels for the Ar Rasfa assemblage are with Middle Levantine Mousterian assemblages. As seen at Naamé, Tabun C, and Qafzeh Cave, such Middle Mousterian assemblages feature wide variation in core preparation methods, albeit with a common focus on the production of large oval Levallois flakes. Scrapers are rare, even in assemblages located far from raw material sources (e.g., Qafzeh)(Hovers 2009).

Assigning Ar Rasfa to the Middle Levantine Mousterian, ca. 75-130 Kya, places it among a group of assemblages that are relatively rare (see Figure 5.1). This would be the first Middle Levantine Mousterian site known from Jordan. On the other hand, Middle Levantine Mousterian assemblages are known from sites in areas contiguous to northwestern Jordan, including northern Israel (Tabun, Qafzeh), Lebanon (Naamé, Nahr Ibrahim/Asfouriyeh Cave, Ksar Akil) and Syria (El Kowm, Douara, Yabrud). At present, no geochronological evidence is available that can either confirm or refute the age implied by this attribution, which therefore must remain a hypothesis to be tested by future research.

Geoisotopic studies of cave speleothems from northern and central Israel dating to this period suggest a hot and humid climate prevailing in the Levant (Almogi-Labin et al. 2004). Under such conditions, it would seem reasonable for humans living in the "rain shadow" of northwestern Jordan to focus their settlement around stable freshwater sources, such as the lower reaches of Wadi Yabis, Wadi Zagh, and the environs of Ar Rasfa. An area with abundant flint, such as Ar Rasfa, would likely have been a place where humans aggregated, knapping stone tools for foraging excursions to higher altitudes.

Middle Levantine Mousterian assemblages are stratigraphically associated with fossil remains of both *Homo sapiens* (at Qafzeh and [arguably] Skhul) and *Homo neanderthalensis* (Tabun C1 and C2). Studies of these assemblages have thus far not revealed clear differences in the ways that *Homo sapiens* and Neandertals made stone tools. This being the case, it is not possible to associate the behavior patterns inferred from the Ar Rasfa evidence solely to one or the other of these hominins. One could argue the case for viewing this evidence as reflecting both Neandertal and *Homo sapiens* activities, but there is thus far no clear evidence that both hominin species were in the Levant at the same time (Shea 2008). The hypothesis that the Ar Rasfa evidence may reflect primitive behavior patterns shared jointly by Neandertals and early *Homo sapiens* is the least problematical hypothesis (Shea 2006b). Structurally similar Middle Paleolithic sites and assemblages (places near water sources where abundant raw materials were knapped into tool blanks) are known from countless localities throughout Europe and Africa (Barham and Mitchell 2008, Gamble 1999), these two hominins' presumed continents of evolutionary origin.

Comparison to Montane Southwest Asian Middle Paleolithic Assemblages

The region nearest to the Levant with the richest and best documented Middle Paleolithic record is the Zagros mountain range, which straddles the political borders

Figure 5.2 Map showing known locations of Middle Paleolithic sites in the Zagros Mountains or Iraq/Iran (modified from map in Lindly 2005).

between Turkey, Iraq and Iran (see Figure 5.2). Lindly (2005) offers the most authoritative recent synthesis of this evidence (see Table 5.1). The most famous of these Zagros Middle Paleolithic sites is Shanidar Cave, from which numerous Neandertal skeletons and thousands of "Zagros Mousterian" stone tools were recovered by the Solecki excavations in the 1950s-1960s (Solecki 1971). Other Middle Paleolithic sites in the Zagros include Barda Balka, Bisitun, Warwasi, Kobeh, Kunji, and Gar Arjeneh (Baumler and Speth 1993, Dibble 1984, Dibble and Holdaway 1993, Lindly 2005, Solecki and Solecki 1993). Many of these sites were excavated in the 1950s-1970s and only published in detail recently.

Many of the ways in which the Ar Rasfa assemblage differs from Zagros Mousterian assemblages are also the ways in which Levantine Mousterian assemblages in general differ from Zagros Mousterian ones. Zagros Mousterian assemblages superficially seem to be similar to at least Later Levantine Mousterian ones in featuring large numbers of points, but the points from Zagros Mousterian assemblages are heavily retouched (Mousterian points, "limaces", and convergent scrapers) while unretouched or minimally-retouched Levallois predominate among most Levantine Mousterian assemblages. In terms of core technology, Levallois cores are rare in Zagros Mousterian assemblages and discoidal cores are common. Discoidal cores are

Table 5.1 Comparison of Levantine and Taurus-Zagros Middle Paleolithic records.

Site types	Levant[1]	Zagros-Taurus[2]
Cave sites	30	>4
Open Air sites	10	1
Lake Edge sites	1	0
Sites with substantial (i.e., non-dental) hominin fossils	6	2
Well-documented zooarchaeological assemblages	>15	2
Predominant core technology	Levallois	Discoidal
Common retouched tools	Simple sidescrapers and endscrapers	Points, convergent scrapers.

Notes: [1] See Shea (2003b), [2] See Lindly (2005)

common in Levantine Mousterian assemblages, but they are usually outnumbered by Levallois cores (as is the case with Ar Rasfa).

Some of the differences between Levantine and Zagros Mousterian assemblages have been argued to reflect differences in raw material provisioning strategies reflecting raw material availability and topographic contrasts (Rolland and Dibble 1990). Many of the Zagros sites are at higher elevations and (at least thought to be) relatively distant from raw material sources. In contrast, few Levantine sites are located more than 10-20 km from high-quality flint sources: in most cases flint sources lie within a few hundred meters (Hovers 2009). A closer, more analogous comparison between Ar Rasfa and Zagros Mousterian assemblages would require well-excavated and documented sites from relatively lower elevations near water and raw material sources. Few such sites are known at present, though Barda Balka, in Iraq, is a possible candidate site. The recent resumption of prehistoric survey in both Iran and Iraq holds out the possibility such sites will be discovered in the near future.

Prospects for Future Research

Excavation and analysis of the Ar Rasfa site and its lithic assemblage raise important questions about the future course of research on the Middle Paleolithic of Jordan, the Levantine Mousterian, and the larger prehistory of Southwest Asia.

Relatively little is known about the Middle Paleolithic of northwestern Jordan. For a variety of reasons (ease of travel, absence of cultivated areas), foreign and Jordanian researchers interested in the Paleolithic period have tended to focus their efforts on the southern part of the country and around the desert oasis at Azraq. This is ironic, because northwestern Jordan is close to, and shares similar ecogeographic features with, those parts of Israel and Palestine and that preserve the richest known Middle Paleolithic sites. To improve the quality of information from northwestern Jordan, it is important for archaeologists to follow up on survey reports (Banning and Fawcett 1983, Macumber 1992, Muheisen 1988, Palumbo et al. 1990) that identify Middle Paleolithic localities in the Jordan Valley

itself as well as in higher elevations. It is true that many caves in the region have been disturbed by pastoralists and by other recent activities, but it is also true that the number of caves and rockshelters currently visible is but a fraction of those that were extant in the past. Many of these caves may now be partly buried and it is possible that geophysical methods of subsurface testing could bring them to light. Areas featuring actively-flowing springs today are a logical focus for such survey, because lower Pleistocene sea levels would have increased spring activity in the past (Bar-Yosef and Vandermeersch 1972), making such areas magnets for human settlements.

Paleolithic archaeology tends to focus its energies on cave/rockshelter sites, but as can be seen from the analysis of the Ar Rasfa assemblage, much can be learned about human behavior from open-air sites as well. Future research on the Middle Paleolithic of northwestern Jordan will naturally focus on caves, but it should also include systematic efforts to find open-air sites preserved in good stratigraphic contexts. In the past, the strongest disincentives for excavating open-air Paleolithic sites were that they did not usually contain organic remains (bones, charcoal) or other materials amenable to geochronometric analysis. Today, however, thermoluminescence dating can be applied to burnt flints (Valladas et al. 1987), and optically-stimulated luminescence dating can be applied to unburnt flints or even to quartz grains in sedimentary deposits (Jacobs and Roberts 2007).

Lake Kinneret (Sea of Galilee/Lake Tiberias) is not within Jordan, but it is close enough that anyone interested in Middle Paleolithic archaeology must pay close attention to the nature of sediments now being exposed there by unprecedented lower lake levels. Reconnaissance and survey along the shores of Lake Kinneret have shown that rich Upper Paleolithic contexts are preserved there, e.g., Ohalo II (Nadel 2002). It is not beyond the realm of possibility that these sediments may contain waterlogged contexts and preserved organic remains like those already known from Middle Pleistocene contexts at Gesher Benot Ya'acov (Goren-Inbar et al. 2002) and in Azraq (Rollefson et al. 1997).

In the Levant, as in much of North Africa and the Arabian

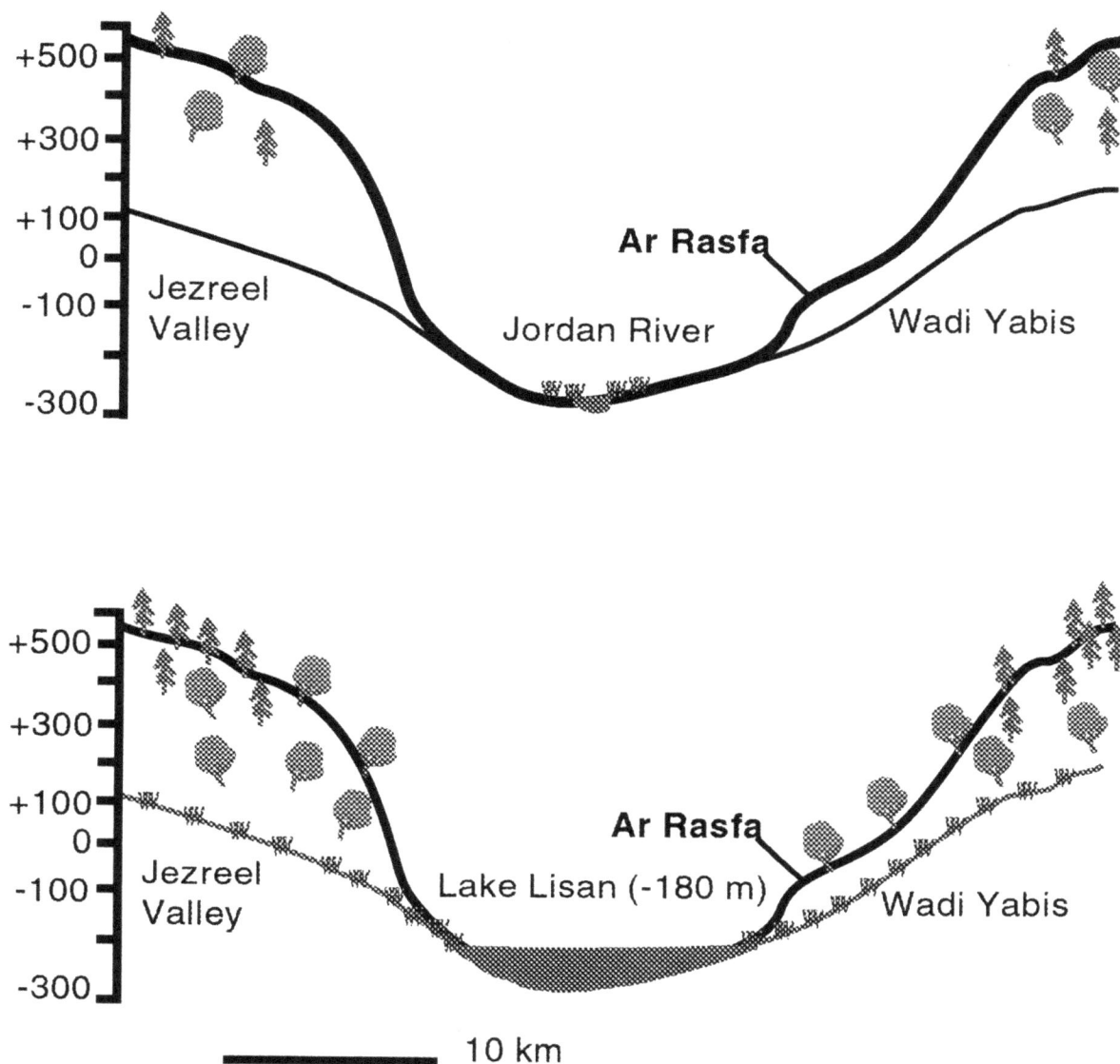

Figure 5.3 Conjectural reconstruction of the Ar Rasfa's position in the northern Jordan Valley under warm humid conditions like those prevailing today (above) and under cold dry conditions in the past (below).

Peninsula, there is a popular aphorism, "water is life". Middle Paleolithic humans either knew this or at least acted as if they did, repeatedly situating their habitation sites near water sources. These sources included springs flowing out of caves as well as sites located near the margins of lakes. Placing habitation sites near the edges of lakes is a settlement pattern that extends back in Levantine prehistory to at least early Middle Pleistocene times, as seen at Gesher Benot Ya'acov (Goren-Inbar et al. 2000), and possibly earlier, as seen at 'Ubeidiya (Bar-Yosef and Tchernov 1972, Shea 1999b). Within the larger scope of research on Levantine Middle Paleolithic settlement patterns, more attention needs to be focused on sites located in perilimnic contexts, in fossilized sand dunes (such as the *kurkar* [calcareous sandstone] deposits along the Israeli Coastal Plain and Gaza Strip, and in preserved lake sediments in the interior parts of the Levant. Middle Paleolithic artifacts have been found in such fossil lake

deposits at Biqat Quneitra (Golan Heights) as well as near El Kowm and Palmyra (Syria), Azraq (Jordan) and Mudawwara (Jordan/Saudi Arabia border). As matters stand today, archaeologists know little about the variability of Middle Paleolithic human activities in and around ancient lakes, even though such lakes would have offered them abundant food resources.

It would be desirable to compare Ar Rasfa, as an open-air Levantine Middle Paleolithic site, to similar sites from nearby regions. The nearest sizable cluster of Middle Paleolithic sites are those from the Zagros-Taurus mountain ranges. Unfortunately, the Middle Paleolithic record of the Zagros-Taurus is known almost exclusively from excavations in caves and rockshelters. Apart from Barda Balka and older (presumably unsystematic) surface collections, there are insufficient open-air sites to allow comparison with Ar Rasfa. With the reconstruction and reconstitution of the Iraq National Museum and Department of Antiquities and the resumption of fieldwork in Iran by the Geological Survey of that country, it is highly likely that additional open-air Middle Paleolithic sites will be discovered in the near future. The documentation of the Ar Rasfa site presented in this study will be a point of comparison for these future discoveries.

"The past is a different country, they do things differently there." This first sentence of Leslie Poles Hartley's novel, *The Go-Between* (1953) captures an essential truth about the Paleolithic Period. It is truly a "lost world" whose human inhabitants behaved in ways that are in some respects familiar and in others utterly alien to us. Pleistocene environments were dramatically different from present-day ones. In Southwest Asia, the landscape was populated by elephant, rhinoceros, hippopotamus, aurochs, Eurasian lion, and other animal species that are now extinct. Plant species common in the Late Pleistocene Levant survive in a few refugia, but today they are mostly found hundreds of kilometers north in Anatolia, the Zagros, and Central Asia (Blondel and Aronson 1999, Qumsiyeh 1996, Zohary 1973). Climate shifted rapidly and unpredictably between cold dry and warm humid conditions (Almogi-Labin et al. 2004, Burroughs 2005). Ar Rasfa is almost ideally situated to allow its human occupants to exploit strategic resources across a wide range of climatic conditions (Figure 5.3). Under warm humid conditions like those prevailing today,

rich riverine habitats would have been a short walk to the west. Woodland resources would have been a bit further distant, a few kilometers upslope to the east. Under cold, dry conditions, when the Lisan paleo-lake filled the Jordan Rift Valley, aquatic resources would have been nearby, and the site would likely have been surrounded by woodland and steppe vegetation. In fact, one of the surprising findings about the site is that there is so little evidence for post-Middle Paleolithic human activity, other than that dating to ethnohistoric times.

To survive in this landscape, humans had to cooperate, and it is virtually certain that the skill with which humans find ways to cooperate today have their evolutionary roots in the Pleistocene. It is easy to forget this, and to think that the countless disagreements that afflict our crowded planet are inevitable consequences of being human. But, there is actually little evidence to support this. The first defensively-walled cities are only 5000 years old. By improving our understanding of Pleistocene humans, how they lived, the challenges they faced, and the strategies they deployed in the face of these challenges, we build a powerful alternative vision of human nature and society. We cannot go back to living the way our species did in Paleolithic times, but we can learn valuable lessons about our species' potential for social, behavioral, and evolutionary change from the modest records of chipped stone tools that our ancestors left behind.

References Cited

Abed, A., P. Carbonel, J. Collina-Girard, M. Fontugne, N. Petit-Maire, J.-C. Reyss, and S. Yasin. 2000. Un paléolac du dernier interglaciare pléistocene dans l'Extreme-Sud hyperaride de la Jordanie. *Comptes Rendus de l'Academie des Science, Paris, Sciences de la Terre et des planètes* 330:259-264.

Akazawa, T. 1987. «The Ecology of the Middle Paleolithic Occupation at Douara Cave, Syria,» in *Paleolithic Site of Douara Cave and Paleogeography of the Palmyra Basin in Syria, Part IV: 1984 Excavations.* Edited by T. Akazawa and Y. Sakaguchi, pp. 155-166. Tokyo: University of Tokyo Museum Bulletin No. 29.

Akazawa, T., and S. Muhesen. Editors. 2003. *Neanderthal Burials. Excavations of the Dederiyeh Cave, Afrin, Syria.* Aukland, New Zealand: KW Publications.

Akazawa, T., and Y. Sakaguchi. Editors. 1987. *Paleolithic Site of the Douara Cave and Paleogeography of the Palymyra Basin in Syria. Part IV: 1984 Excavations.* Tokyo: University of Tokyo Museum Bulletin No. 29.

Almogi-Labin, A., M. Bar-Matthews, and A. Ayalon. 2004. "Climate Variability in the Levant and Northeast Africa during the Late Quaternary Based on Marine and Land Records," in *Human Paleoecology in the Levantine Corridor.* Edited by N. Goren-Inbar and J. Speth, pp. 117-134. Oxford, UK: Oxbow Books.

Alperson-Afil, N., and E. Hovers. 2005. Differential Use of Space in the Neandertal Site of Amud Cave, Israel. *Eurasian Prehistory* 3:3-22.

Andrefsky, W. J. 2005. *Lithics: Macroscopic Approaches to Analysis, Second Edition.* New York: Cambridge University Press.

Antón, S., and C. C. Swisher, III. 2004. Early Dispersals of Homo from Africa. *Annual Review of Anthropology* 33:271-296.

Bahn, P. G., and J. Vertut. 1997. *Journey Through the Ice Age.* Berkeley: University of California Press.

Banning, E. B., and C. Fawcett. 1983. Man-Land Relationships in the Ancient Wadi Ziqlab: Report of the 1981 Survey. *Annual of the Department of Antiquities of Jordan* 27:291-309.

Bar-Yosef, O. 2000. "The Middle and Early Upper Paleolithic in Southwest Asia and Neighboring Regions," in *The Geography of Neandertals and Modern Humans in Europe and the Greater Mediterranean.* Edited by O. Bar-Yosef and D. Pilbeam, pp. 107-156. Cambridge, MA: Peabody Museum of Archaeology and Ethnology, Bulletin No. 8.

Bar-Yosef, O., and N. Goren-Inbar. 1993. *The Lithic Assemblages of 'Ubeidiya. Qedem 34.* Jerusalem: Hebrew University Institute of Archaeology.

Bar-Yosef, O., and L. Meignen. Editors. 2008. *Kebara Cave, Mt. Carmel, Israel: The Middle and Upper Paleolithic Archaeology Part I.* Cambridge, MA: Peabody Museum of Archaeology and Ethnology, Harvard University (American School of Prehistoric Research Bulletin 49).

Bar-Yosef, O., and E. Tchernov. 1972. *On the Palaeo-Ecological History of the Site of 'Ubeidiya.* Jerusalem: Israel Academy of Sciences.

Bar-Yosef, O., and B. Vandermeersch. 1972. "The stratigraphical and cultural problems of the passage from Middle to Upper Paleolithic in Palestinian caves," in *The Origin of Homo sapiens/Origine de l'homme modern.* Edited by F. Bordes, pp. 221-225. Paris: UNESCO.

—. 1993. Modern Humans in the Levant. *Scientific American* 268:94-100.

Barham, L., and P. Mitchell. 2008. *The First Africans: African Archaeology from the Earliest Toolmakers to Most Recent Foragers.* New York: Cambridge University Press.

Baumler, M. F., and J. D. Speth. 1993. "A Middle Paleolithic Assemblage from Kunji Cave, Iran," in *The Paleolithic Prehistory of the Zagros-Taurus.* Edited by D. Olzewski and H. L. Dibble, pp. 1-73. Philadelphia, PA: University of Pennsylvania Museum (Monograph No. 83).

Bender, F. 1974. *Geology of Jordan.* Berlin: Gebrüder Borntraeger.

Binford, L. R. 1979. Organization and Formation Processes: Looking at Curated Technologies. *Journal of Anthropological Research* 35:255-273.

—. 1986. An Alyawara Day: Making Men's Knives and Beyond. *American Antiquity* 51:547-562.

Binford, S. R. 1966. Me'arat Shovakh (Mugharet es-Shubbabiq). *Israel Exploration Journal* 16:18-32, 96-113.

—. 1968. Early Upper Pleistocene Adaptations in the Levant. *American Anthropologist* 70:707-717.

—. 1970. Late Middle Paleolithic Adaptations and Their Possible Consequences. *Biosciences* 20:280-283.

Bisson, M. S. 2000. Nineteenth Century Tools for Twenty-First Century Archaeology? Why the Middle Paleolithic Typology of François Bordes Must Be Replaced. *Journal of Archaeological Method and Theory* 7:1-48.

Bleed, P. 1986. The Optimal Design of Hunting Weapons: Maintainability or Reliability? *American Antiquity* 51:737-747.

Blondel, J., and J. Aronson. 1999. *Biology and Wildlife of the Mediterranean Region.* New York: Oxford University Press.

Boëda, E., L. Bourguignon, and C. Griggo. 1998. "Activités de subsistance au Paléolithique moyen: couche V13B' du gisement d'Umm el Tlel (Syrie)," in *Economie préhistorique: les comportements de subsistance au Paléolithique.* Edited by J.-P. Brugal, L. Meignen, and M. Patou-Mathis, pp. 243-259. Sophia Antipolis, France: Editions APDCA.

Boëda, E., J.-M. Geneste, C. Griggo, N. Mercier, S. Muhesen, J. L. Reyss, A. Taha, and H. Valladas. 1999. A Levallois point embedded in the vertebra of a wild ass (Equus africanus): Hafting, projectiles and Mousterian hunting weapons. *Antiquity* 73:394-402.

Boëda, E., J.-M. Geneste, and L. Meignen. 1990. Identification de chaines opératoires lithiques du Paléolithique ancien et moyen. *Paleo* 2:43-80.

Boëda, E., and S. Muhesen. 1993. Umm el Tlel (El Kowm, Syrie): Étude préliminaire des industries du paléolithique moyen et supérieur. *Cahiers de l'Euphrates* 7:47-91.

Bordes, F. 1961. *Typologie du Paléolithique ancien et moyen.* Bordeaux: Delmas.

Brantingham, P. J., A. J. Krivoshapkin, L. Jinzheng, and Y. Tserendagva. 2001. The Initial Upper Paleolithic of Northeast Asia. *Current Anthropology* 42:735-747.

Brose, D. S., and M. H. Wolpoff. 1970. Early Upper Paleolithic Man and Middle Paleolithic Tools. *American Anthropologist* 73:1156-1194.

Burroughs, W. J. 2005. *Climate Change in Prehistory: The End of the Reign of Chaos.* Cambridge, UK: Cambridge University Press.

Callander, J. 2004. Dorothy Garrod's excavations in the Late Mousterian of Shukbah Cave, Palestine reconsidered. *Procedings of the Prehistoric Society* 70:207-231.

Cann, J. R., J. E. Dixon, and C. Renfrew. 1969. "Obsidian analysis and the obsidian trade," in *Science in archaeology. A survey of progress and research.* Edited by D. Brothwell and E. Higgs, pp. 578-591. London: Thames and Hudson.

Chase, P. G. 1991. Symbols and Paleolithic artifacts: style, standardization, and the imposition of arbitrary form. *Journal of Anthropological Archaeology* 10:193-214.

Chazan, M. 1997. Redefining Levallois. *Journal of Human Evolution* 33:719-735.

Clark, G. A., and J. Lindly. 1988. The biocultural transition and the origin of modern humans in the Levant. *Paléorient* 14:159-167.

Clark, G. A., J. Schuldenrein, M. L. Donaldson, H. P. Schwarcz, W. J. Rink, and S. K. Fish. 1997. "Chronostratigraphic Contexts of Middle Paleolithic Horizons at the 'Ain Difla Rockshelter (WHS 634), West-Central Jordan," in *The Prehistory of Jordan, II. Perspectives from 1997.* Edited by H.-G. K. Gebel, Z. Kafafi, and G. Rollefson, pp. 77-100. Berlin: ex oriente.

Coon, C. S. 1957. *The Seven Caves.* New York: Alfred A. Knopf.

Copeland, L. 1975. "The Middle and Upper Palaeolithic of Lebanon and Syria in the light of recent research," in *Problems in Prehistory: North Africa and the Levant.* Edited by F. Wendorf and A. E. Marks, pp. 317-350. Dallas: SMU Press.

—. 1983. "The Levalloiso-Mousterian of Bezez Cave Level B.," in *Adlun in the Stone Age*, vol. 2. Edited by D. A. Roe, pp. 261-324. Oxford, UK: British Archaeological Reports International Series 159(i).

—. 1988. Environment, Chronology, and Lower-Middle Paleolithic Occupation of the Azraq Basin, Jordan. *Paléorient* 14:66-75.

—. 1998. "The Middle Palaeolithic Flint Industry of Ras el-Kelb," in *The Mousterian Site of Ras el-Kelb, Lebanon.* Edited by L. Copeland and N. Moloney, pp. 73-175. Oxford: British Archaeological Reports, BAR International Series, No. 706.

Cordova, C., C. Foley, A. Nowell, and M. Bisson. 2004. Landforms, Sediments, Soil Development, and Prehistoric Site Settings on the Madaba-Dhiban Plateau, Jordan. *Geoarchaeology* 20:29-56.

Crew, H. 1976. "The Mousterian Site of Rosh Ein Mor," in *Prehistory and Paleoenvironments in the Central Negev, Israel, Vol. 1.* Edited by A. E. Marks, pp. 75-112. Dallas: Southern Methodist University Press.

Cziesla, E. 1990. "On refitting stone artefacts," in *The Big Puzzle: International Symposium on Refitting Stone Implements.* Edited by E. Cziesla, S. Eickhoff, N. Arts, and D. Winter, pp. 9-44. Bonn: Holos Press.

d'Errico, F. 2003. The Invisible Frontier. A Multiple Species Model for the Origin of Behavioral Modernity. *Evolutionary Anthropology* 12:188-202.

Davis, Z. J. 1999. Levantine Mousterian mobility patterns: the view from Mt. Carmel. *Journal of Human Evolution* 36:A6.

—. 2000. "Costs and Benefits of Levallois Flake Production: An Economic Perspective on the Variability in Middle Paleolithic Stone Tool Assemblages." *Abstracts of the 65th Annual Meeting of the Society for American Archaeology, Philadelphia, PA, 2000,* pp. 102-103.

Davis, Z. J., and J. J. Shea. 1998. Quantifying lithic curation: An experimental test of Dibble and Pelcin's original flake-tool mass predictor. *Journal of Archaeological Science* 25:603-610.

Debénath, A., and H. L. Dibble. 1994. *Handbook of Paleolithic Typology, Vol. 1: Lower and Middle Paleolithic of Europe.* Philadelphia: University of Pennsylvania Press.

Dennell, R. 2009. *The Palaeolithic Settlement of Asia.* Cambridge University Press: Cambridge, UK.

Dibble, H., and S. McPherron. 2007. The Lower/Middle Paleolithic Periodization in Western Europe. *Current Anthropology* 47:777-803.

Dibble, H. L. 1984. The Mousterian Industry from Bisitun

Cave (Iran). *Paléorient* 10:23-34.

—. 1991. Mousterian Assemblage Variability on an Interregional Scale. *Journal of Anthropological Research* 47:239-258.

—. 1995. Middle Paleolithic Scraper Reduction: Background, Clarification, and Review of the Evidence to Date. *Journal of Archaeological Method and Theory* 2:299-368.

—. 1997. Platform variability and flake morphology: A comparison of experimental and archaeological data and implications for interpreting prehistoric lithic technological strategies. *Lithic Technology* 22:150-170.

Dibble, H. L., and M. C. Bernard. 1980. A Comparative Study of Edge Angle Measurement Techniques. *American Antiquity* 45:857-865.

Dibble, H. L., and S. J. Holdaway. 1993. "The Middle Paleolithic Industries of Warwasi," in *The Paleolithic Prehistory of the Zagros-Taurus*. Edited by D. Olzewski and H. L. Dibble, pp. 75-99. Philadelphia, PA: University of Pennsylvania Museum (Monograph No. 83).

Domínguez-Rodrigo, M., and T. R. Pickering. 2003. Early Hominid Hunting and Scavenging: A Zooarchaeological Review. *Evolutionary Anthropology* 12:275-282.

Eren, M. I., M. Dominguez-Rodrigo, S. L. Kuhn, D. S. Adler, I. Le, and O. Bar-Yosef. 2005. Defining and measuring reduction in unifacial stone tools. *Journal of Archaeological Science* 32:1190-1201.

Eren, M. I., A. Greenspan, and C. G. Sampson. 2008. Are Upper Paleolithic blade cores more productive than Middle Paleolithic discoidal cores? A replication experiment. *Journal of Human Evolution* 55:952-961.

Feblot-Augustins, J. 1997. *La Circulation des matières premiers au Paléolithique: Synthése de données, perspectives comportementales*. Liège: Etudes et Recherches Archéologiques de l'Université de Liège, No. 75.

Fleisch, H. 1970. Les habitats du paléolithique moyen à Naamé (Liban). *Bulletin de la Musée de Beyrouth* 23:25-93.

Foley, R. 1987. *Another unique species: patterns in human evolutionary ecology*. Harlow, UK: Longman Group.

Foley, R., and M. M. Lahr. 1997. Mode 3 Technologies and the Evolution of Modern Humans. *Cambridge Archaeological Journal* 7:3-36.

Gamble, C. 1999. *The Palaeolithic Societies of Europe*. New York: Cambridge University Press.

—. 2007. *Origins and Revolutions: Human Identity in Earliest Prehistory*. New York, NY: Cambridge University Press.

Garrod, D. A. E. 1937a. "Et-Tabun: Description and Archaeology," in *The Stone Age of Mount Carmel, Vol. 1: Excavations in the Wady el-Mughara*. Edited by D. A. E. Garrod and D. Bate, pp. 57-70. Oxford, UK: Clarendon Press.

—. 1937b. "Mugharet El Wad " in *The Stone Age of Mount Carmel, Vol. 1: Excavations in the Wady el-Mughara*. Edited by D. A. E. Garrod and D. Bate, pp. 3-55. Oxford, UK: Clarendon Press.

Geneste, J.-M. 1985. Analyse lithique d'industries moustériennes du Périgord: approche technologique du comportement des groupes humaine au Paléolithique

moyen. Ph. D. thesis, Université de Bordeaux.

Gilead, I., and C. Grigson. 1984. Far'ah II: A Middle Palaeolithic open-air site in the Northern Negev, Israel. *Proceedings of the Prehistoric Society* 50:71-97.

Gisis, I., and O. Bar-Yosef. 1974. New Excavations in Zuttiyeh Cave. *Paléorient* 2:175-180.

Goldberg, P. 1995. "The Changing Landscape," in *Archaeology of Society in the Holy Land*. Edited by T. E. Levy, pp. 40-57. New York: Facts on File.

Goren-Inbar, N. Editor. 1990. *Quneitra: A Mousterian Site on the Golan Heights*. Jerusalem: Hebrew University Institute of Archaeology (Qedem No. 31).

Goren-Inbar, N., C. S. Feibel, K. L. Verosub, Y. Melamed, M. E. Kislev, E. Tchernov, and I. Saragusti. 2000. Pleistocene Milestones on the Out-of-Africa Corrdor at Gesher Benot Ya'aqov, Israel. *Science* 289:944-947.

Goren-Inbar, N., E. Werker, and C. S. Feibel. Editors. 2002. *The Acheulian Site of Gesher Benot Ya'acov, Israel: The Wood Assemblage*. Oxford, UK: Oxbow Books.

Gould, R. A. 1980. *Living Archaeology*. Cambridge, UK: Cambridge University Press.

Gould, R. A., D. A. Koster, and A. Sontz. 1971. The Lithic Assemblage of the Western Desert Aborigines of Australia. *American Antiquity* 36:149-168.

Gould, S. J., and R. C. Lewontin. 1979. The spandrels of San Marco and the Panglossian paradigm: a critique of the adaptationist programme. *Proceedings of the Royal Society of London* 205:581-598.

Guthrie, R. D. 2005. *The Nature of Paleolithic Art*. Chicago, IL: University of Chicago Press.

Hayden, B. 1979. *Palaeolithic Reflections: Lithic Technology and Ethnographic Excavations among Australian Aborigines*. Canberra: Australian Institute of Aboriginal Studies.

Hayden, B., and M. W. Nelson. 1981. The Use of Chipped Lithic Material in the Contemporary Maya Highlands. *American Antiquity* 46:885-898.

Henry, D. O. 1982. "Paleolithic adaptive strategies in southern Jordan: Results of the 1979 field season," in *Studies in the History and Archaeology of Jordan I*. Edited by A. Hadidi, pp. 55-58. Amman: Department of Antiquities, Jordan.

—. 1995a. "The influence of mobility levels on Levallois point production, Late Levantine Mousterian, Southern Jordan," in *The Definition and Interpretation of Levallois Technology*. Edited by H. L. Dibble and O. Bar-Yosef, pp. 185-200. Madison, WI: Prehistory Press.

—. 1995b. "The Middle Paleolithic Sites," in *Prehistoric Cultural Ecology and Evolution: Insights from Southern Jordan*. Edited by D. O. Henry, pp. 49-84. New York: Plenum.

—. 1998. "The Middle Paleolithic of Jordan," in *The Prehistoric Archaeology of Jordan, BAR International Series 705*. Edited by D. O. Henry, pp. 23-39. Oxford, UK: British Archaeological Reports.

—. Editor. 2003. *Neanderthals in the Levant: Behavioral Organization and the Beginnings of Human Modernity*. New York: Continuum.

Henry, D. O., H. J. Hietala, A. M. Rosen, Y. Demidenko, V. Usik, and T. L. Armagan. 2004. Human Behavioral Organization in the Middle Paleolithic: Were

Neanderthals Different? *American Anthropologist* 106:17-31.

Hoffecker, J. F. 2004. *A Prehistory of the North: Human Settlement of the Higher Latitudes.* Piscataway, NJ: Rutgers University Press.

Horowitz, A. 1987. Subsurface palynostratigraphy and paleoclimates of the Quaternary Jordan Rift Valley Fill, Israel. *Israel Journal of Earth Sciences* 36:31-44.

Hovers, E. 2004. "Cultural Ecology at the Neandertal Site of Amud Cave, Israel," in *Archaeology and Paleoecology of Eurasia: Papers in Honor of Vadim Ranov.* Edited by A. P. Derevianko and T. I. Nokhrina, pp. 218231. Novosibirsk, Russia: Insititute of Archaeology and Ethnography SB RAS Press.

—. 2006. "Neanderthals and Modern Humans in the Middle Paleolithic of the Levant: What Kind of Interaction?," in *Neanderthals and Moderns Meet.* Edited by N. Conard, pp. 65-85. Tübingen: Kerns Verlag.

—. 2007. "The many faces of cores-on-flakes: a perspective from the Levantine Mousterian," in *Tools versus Cores: Alternative Approaches to Stone Tool Analysis.* Edited by M. S. P., pp. 42-73. Newcastle: Cambridge Scholars Press.

—. 2009. *The Organization of Lithic Technology in the Mousterian Layers of Qafzeh Cave.* Oxford: Oxford University Press.

Howell, F. C. 1958. "Upper Pleistocene Men of the Southwest Asian Mousterian," in *Hundert Jahre Neanderthaler.* Edited by G. H. R. von Koenigswald, pp. 185-198. Utrecht: Kemik en zoon.

—. 1959. Upper Pleistocene stratigraphy and early man in the Levant. *Proceedings of the American Philosophical Society* 103:1-65.

Hublin, J.-J. 2000. "Modern-Nonmodern Hominid Interactions: A Mediterranean Perspective," in *The Geography of Neandertals and Modern Humans in Europe and the Greater Mediterranean.* Edited by O. Bar-Yosef and D. Pilbeam, pp. 157-182. Cambridge, MA: Peabody Museum of Archaeology and Ethnology, Bulletin No. 8.

Inizan, M.-L., M. Reduron-Ballinger, H. Roche, and J. Tixier. 1999. *Technology and Terminology of Knapped Stone (translated by J. Féblot-Augustins). Préhistoire de la Pierre Taillée, Tome 5.* Meudon, FR: Cercle de Recherches et d'Etudes Préhistoriques (CNRS).

Isaac, G. L. 1981. «Stone Age Visiting Cards: Approaches to the Study of Early Land-use Patterns,» in *Past in Perspective.* Edited by I. Hodder, G. Isaac, and N. Hammond, pp. 131-155. Cambridge: Cambridge University Press.

Jacobs, Z., and R. Roberts. 2007. Advances in Optically Stimulated Luminescence Dating of Individual Grains of Quartz from Archaeological Deposits. *Evolutionary Anthropology* 16:204-210.

Jelinek, A. J. 1977. A Preliminary Study of Flakes from the Tabun Cave, Mount Carmel. *Eretz-Israel* 13 (Stekelis Memorial Volume):87-96.

—. 1981. "The Middle Paleolithic of the Southern Levant from the Perspective of Tabun Cave," in *Préhistoire du Levant.* Edited by J. Cauvin and P. Sanlaville, pp. 265-280. Paris: Editions du CNRS.

—. 1982a. "The Middle Paleolithic in the Southern Levant with comments on the appearance of modern Homo sapiens," in *The Transition from Lower to Middle Paleolithic and the Origins of Modern Man.* Edited by A. Ronen, pp. 57-104. Oxford: British Archaeological Reports International Series 151.

—. 1982b. The Tabun Cave and Paleolithic Man in the Levant. *Science* 216:1369-1375.

Kaufman, D. 1999. *Archaeological Perspectives on the Origins of Modern Humans: A View from the Levant.* Westport, CT: Bergin & Garvey.

Klein, R. G. 2008. Out of Africa and the Evolution of Human Behavior. *Evolutionary Anthropology* 17:267-281.

—. 2009. *The Human Career, 3rd Edition.* Chicago: University of Chicago Press.

Knecht, H. 1994. Late Ice Age Hunting Technology. *Scientific American* 271:82-87.

Kramer, A., T. L. Crummett, and M. H. Wolpoff. 2001. Out of Africa and into the Levant: Replacement or admixture in Western Asia. *Quaternary International* 75:51-63.

Kuhn, S. L. 1990. A geometrical index of reduction for unifacial stone tools. *Journal of Archaeological Science* 17:583-593.

—. 1995. *Mousterian Lithic Technology: An Ecological Perspective.* Princeton, NJ: Princeton University Press.

Kuhn, S. L., and M. C. Stiner. 2001. "The Antiquity of Hunter-Gatherers," in *Hunter-Gatherers: An Interdisciplinary Perspective.* Edited by C. Panter-Brick, R. H. Layton, and P. Rowley-Conwy, pp. 99-142. Cambridge, UK: Cambridge University Press.

Le Tensorer, J.-M. 2004. "Nouvelles fouilles à Hummal (El Kowm, Syrie centrale) premiers résultats (1997-2001)," in *From the River to the Sea The Paleolithic and the Neolithic on the Euphrates and in the Northern Levant. Studies in honour of Lorraine Copeland.* Edited by O. Aurenche, M. Le Mière, and P. Sanlaville, pp. 223-240. Oxford, UK: British Archaeological Reports International Series S1263.

Le Tensorer, J.-M., R. Jagher, P. Rentzel, T. Hauck, K. Ismail-Meyer, C. Pümpin, and D. Wojtczak. 2007. Long-Term Site Formation Processes at the Natural Springs Nadaouiyeh and Hummal in the El Kowm Oasis, Central Syria. *Geoarchaeology* 22:621-639.

Leakey, M. D. 1971. *Olduvai Gorge: Excavations in Beds I and II, 1960-1963.* Cambridge: Cambridge University Press.

Leroi-Gourhan, A. 1943. *Evolution et Techniques: L'Homme et La Matiere.* Paris, FR: Éditions Albin Michel.

Lindly, J., and G. A. Clark. 1987. A Preliminary Lithic Analysis of the Mousterian Site of 'Ain Difla (WHS Site 634) in the Wadi Ali, West-Central Jordan. *Proceedings of the Prehistoric Society* 53:279-292.

Lindly, J. M. 2005. *The Mousterian of the Zagros: A Regional Perspective.* Tempe, AZ: Arizona State University (Anthropological Research Papers, No. 56).

Macumber, P. G. 1992. The Geological Setting of Palaeolithic sites at Tabaqat Fahl, Jordan. *Paléorient* 18:31-43.

Marean, C. W. 2007. "Heading North: An Africanist

Perspective on the Replacement of Neanderthals by Modern Humans," in *Rethinking the Human Revolution*. Edited by P. Mellars, K. Boyle, O. Bar-Yosef, and C. Stringer, pp. 367-382. Cambridge, UK: McDonald Institute for Archaeological Research Monographs.

Marks, A., and P. Volkman. 1986. The Mousterian of Ksar Akil: Levels XXVIA through XXVIIIB. *Paléorient* 12:5-20.

McBrearty, S. 2007. "Down with the Revolution," in *Rethinking the Human Revolution*. Edited by P. Mellars, K. Boyle, O. Bar-Yosef, and C. Stringer, pp. 133-152. Cambridge, UK: McDonald Institute for Archaeological Research Monographs.

McBrearty, S., and A. S. Brooks. 2000. The Revolution That Wasn't: a New Interpretation of the Origin of Modern Human Behavior. *Journal of Human Evolution* 39:453-563.

McCown, T. D. 1937. "Mugharet es-Skhul. Description and Excavations.," in *The Stone Age of Mount Carmel, Vol. 1: Excavations in the Wady el-Mughara*. Edited by D. Garrod and D. M. A. Bate, pp. 91-112. Oxford: Clarendon Press.

Meignen, L. 1988. Le Paléolithique moyen du Levant: Synthese. *Paléorient* 14:168-173.

—. 1998. "Hayonim Cave Lithic Assemblages in the Context of the Near Eastern Middle Paleolithic: A Preliminary Report," in *Neandertals and Modern Humans in Western Asia*. Edited by T. Akazawa, K. Aoki, and O. Bar-Yosef, pp. 165-180. New York: Plenum.

Meignen, L., and O. Bar-Yosef. 1988. "Variabilité Technologique au Proche Orient: l'Example de Kebara," in *L'Homme de Néanderthal, Vol 4: La Téchnique*. Edited by M. Otte, pp. 81-95. Liège: Université de Liège (ERAUL No. 21).

—. 1992. «Middle Paleolithic Lithic Variability in Kebara Cave, Mount Carmel, Israel,» in *The Evolution and Dispersal of Modern Humans in Asia*. Edited by T. Akazawa, K. Aoki, and T. Kimura, pp. 129-148. Tokyo: Hokusen-sha.

Mellars, P. 1994. "The Upper Paleolithic Revolution," in *The Oxford Illustrated Prehistory of Europe*. Edited by B. Cunliffe, pp. 42-78. New York: Oxford University Press.

—. 2005. The Impossible Coincidence. A Single-Species Model for the Origins of Modern Human Behavior in Europe. *Evolutionary Anthropology* 14:12-17.

Monnier, G. 2007. The Lower/Middle Paleolithic Periodization in Western Europe. *Current Anthropology* 47:709-744.

Muheisen, M. 1988. "A Survey of Prehistoric Sites in the Jordan Valley (1985)," in *The Prehistory of Jordan: The State of Research in 1986*. Edited by A. N. Garrard and H. G. Gebel, pp. 503-523. Oxford, UK: British Archaeological Reports International Series 396 (ii).

Munday, F. C. 1976. "Nahal Aqev (D35): A stratified, open-air Mousterian Occupation in the Avdat/Aqev Area," in *Prehistory and Paleoenvironments in the Central Negev, Israel, Vol. 2: The Avdat/Aqev Area, Part 2 and the Har Harif*. Edited by A. E. Marks, pp. 35-60. Dallas: Southern Methodist University Press.

—. 1979. Levantine Mousterian technological variability: A

perspective from the Negev. *Paléorient* 5:87-104.

Nadel, D. Editor. 2002. *Ohalo II, A 23,000-Year-Old Fisher-Hunter-Gatherers' Camp on the Shore of the Sea of Galilee*. Haifa, Israel: Reuben and Edith Hecht Museum, University of Haifa.

Neuville, R. 1934. Le Préhistorique de Palestine. *Revue Biblique* 43:237-259.

Nishiaki, Y., and L. Copeland. 1992. "Keoue Cave, Northern Lebanon, and Its Place in the Context of the Levantine Mousterian," in *The Evolution and Dispersal of Modern Humans in Asia*. Edited by T. Akazawa, K. Aoki, and T. Kimura, pp. 107-128. Tokyo: Hokusen-sha.

Odell, G. H. 2000. Stone Tool Research at the End of the Millennium: Procurement and Technology. *Journal of Archaeological Research* 9:269-331.

—. 2004. *Lithic Analysis*. New York: Kluwer.

Ohnuma, K. 1992. "The significance of Layer B (Square 8-19) of the Amud Cave (Israel) in the Levantine Levalloiso-Mousterian: A technological study," in *The Evolution and Dispersal of Modern Humans in Asia*. Edited by T. Akazawa, K. Aoki, and T. Kimura, pp. 83-106. Tokyo: Hokusen-sha.

Palumbo, G., J. Mabry, and I. Kuijt. 1990. The Wadi el-Yabis Survey: Report on the 1989 Field Season. *Annual of the Department of Antiquities of Jordan* 34:95-118.

Parry, W. A., and R. L. Kelly. 1987. "Expedient Core Technology and Sedentism," in *The Organization of Core Technology*. Edited by J. K. Johnson and C. A. Morrow, pp. 285-304. Boulder, CO: Westview Press.

Pelcin, A. W. 1997. The formation of flakes: The role of platform thickness and exterior platform angle in the production of flake initiations and terminations. *Journal of Archaeological Science* 24:1107-1113.

Phillips, J. L., and I. N. Saca. 2002. Recent excavations at the site of Erq-el-Ahmar. *Antiquity* 76:17-18.

Potts, R. 1988. *Early Hominid Activities at Olduvai*. New York: Aldine de Gruyter.

Quintero, L., P. Wilke, and G. Rollefson. 2004. The Eastern Levant, the Pleistocene, and Paleoanthropology. *ACOR Newsletter* 16:1-3.

Qumsiyeh, M. B. 1996. *Mammals of the Holy Land*. Lubbock, TX: Texas Tech University Press.

Richards, M. P., R. Jacobi, J. Cook, P. B. Pettitt, and C. B. U.-h. w. s. c. s. a. B. W.-G.-c. b. c. f. d. d. a. d. Stringer. 2005. Isotope evidence for the intensive use of marine foods by Late Upper Palaeolithic humans. *Journal of Human Evolution* 49:390-394.

Rolland, N., and H. L. Dibble. 1990. A New Synthesis of Middle Paleolithic Variability. *American Antiquity* 55:480-499.

Rollefson, G., D. Schnurrenberger, L. Quintero, R. Watson, and R. Low. 1997. "'Ain Soda and 'Ain Qasiya: New Late Pleistocene and Early Holocene Sites in the Azraq Shishan Area, Eastern Jordan.," in *The Prehistory of Jordan, II. Perspectives from 1997*. Edited by H.-G. K. Gebel, Z. Kafafi, and G. Rollefson, pp. 45-58. Berlin: ex oriente.

Ronen, A. 1974. *Tirat Carmel: A Mousterian Open-Air Site in Israel*. Tel Aviv: Tel Aviv University Institute of Archaeology, Publication No. 3.

—. 1979. "Paleolithic Industries," in *The Quaternary of*

Israel. Edited by A. Horowitz, pp. 296-307. New York: Academic Press.

——. Editor. 1984. *Sefunim Prehistoric Sites, Mount Carmel, Israel*. Oxford: British Archaeological Reports International Series 230.

Rust, A. 1950. *Die Höhlenfunde von Jabrud (Syrien)*. Neumünster: K. Wacholtz.

Sandgathe, D. M. 2004. Alternative Interpretations of the Levallois Reduction Technique. *Lithic Technology* 29:147-159.

Schroeder, B. 1969. The Lithic Industries from Jerf 'Ajla and Their Bearing on the Problem of a Middle to Upper Paleolithic Transition. Ph.D. Dissertation, Columbia University, New York.

Semenov, S. A. 1964. *Prehistoric Technology*. London: Corey Adams Mackay.

Shea, J. J. 1988. Spear Points from the Middle Paleolithic of the Levant. *Journal of Field Archaeology* 15:441-450.

——. 1989a. "A functional Study of the Lithic Industries Associated with Hominid Fossils in the Kebara and Qafzeh Caves, Israel," in *The Human Revolution: Behavioural and Biological Perspectives on the Origins of Modern Humans*. Edited by P. Mellars and C. Stringer, pp. 611-625. Edinburgh: Edinburgh University Press.

——. 1989b. Tool Use in the Levantine Mousterian of Kebara Cave, Mount Carmel. *Mitekufat HaEven (Journal of the Israel Prehistoric Society)* 22:15-30.

——. 1991. The Behavioral Significance of Levantine Mousterian Industrial Variability. Doctoral Dissertation, Harvard University.

——. 1995a. "Behavioral Factors affecting the Production of Levallois Points in the Levantine Mousterian," in *The Definition and Interpretation of Levallois Technology*. Edited by H. L. Dibble and O. Bar-Yosef, pp. 279-292. Madison, WI: Prehistory Press Monographs in World Archaeology No. 23.

——. 1995b. "Lithic Microwear Analysis of Tor Faraj Rockshelter," in *Prehistoric Ecology and Evolution: Insights from Southern Jordan*. Edited by D. O. Henry, pp. 85-97. New York: Plenum.

——. 1997. "Middle Paleolithic spear point technology," in *Projectile Technology*. Edited by H. Knecht, pp. 79-106. New York: Plenum.

——. 1999a. Ar Rasfa, A Levantine Mousterian Site from Northwest Jordan: A Preliminary Report. *Paléorient* 24:71-78.

——. 1999b. Artifact abrasion, fluvial processes, and "Living Floors" at the Early Paleolithic site of 'Ubeidiya (Jordan Valley, Israel). *Geoarchaeology* 14:191-207.

——. 2001. The Middle Paleolithic: Neandertals and Early Modern Humans in the Levant. *Near Eastern Archaeology* 63:38-64.

——. 2003a. Neandertals, Competition, and the Origin of Modern Human Behavior in the Levant. *Evolutionary Anthropology* 12:173-187.

——. 2003b. The Middle Paleolithic of the East Mediterranean Levant. *Journal of World Prehistory* 17:313-394.

——. 2006a. Child's play: Reflections on the invisibility of children in the paleolithic record. *Evolutionary Anthropology* 15:212-216.

——. 2006b. "The Middle Paleolithic of the Levant: Recursion and Convergence," in *Transitions Before the Transition: Evolution and Stability in the Middle Paleolithic and Middle Stone Age*. Edited by E. Hovers and S. L. Kuhn, pp. 189-212. New York: Plenum/Kluwer.

——. 2006c. The origins of lithic projectile point technology: evidence from Africa, the Levant, and Europe. *Journal of Archaeological Science* 33:823-846.

——. 2007a. "Lithic Archaeology, or, What Stone Tools Can (and Can't) Tell Us About Early Hominin Diets," in *Evolution of the Human Diet: The Known, the Unknown and the Unknowable*. Edited by P. Ungar, pp. 321-351. Oxford, UK: Oxford University Press.

——. 2007b. Microwear Analysis of the Lithic Assemblages associated with Middle Paleolithic *Homo sapiens* in Qafzeh Cave Levels XV-XXIV. *Journal of the Israel Prehistoric Society* 37:5-35.

——. 2007c. "The Boulevard of Broken Dreams: Evolutionary Discontinuity in the Late Pleistocene Levant," in *Rethinking the Human Revolution*. Edited by P. Mellars, K. Boyle, O. Bar-Yosef, and C. Stringer, pp. 219-232. Cambridge, UK: McDonald Institute for Archaeological Research Monographs.

——. 2008. Transitions or turnovers? Climatically-forced extinctions of Homo sapiens and Neanderthals in the East Mediterranean Levant. *Quaternary Science Reviews* 27:2253-2270.

Shea, J. J., and O. Bar-Yosef. 1999. Lithic Assemblages from the New (1988-1994) Excavations at 'Ubeidiya: A Preliminary Report. *Mitekufat HaEven (Journal of the Israel Prehistoric Society)* 28:5-20.

Shea, J. J., and P. L. Crawford. 2003. Middle Paleolithic Northwestern Jordan, 1999 Season: Investigations in Wadi Yabis and Wadi Kufrinja. *Annual of the Department of Antiquities of Jordan* 47:431-441.

Shea, J. J., J. G. Fleagle, and Z. Assefa. 2007. "Context and Chronology of early Homo sapiens fossils from the Omo Kibish Formation, Ethiopia," in *Rethinking the Human Revolution*. Edited by P. Mellars, K. Boyle, O. Bar-Yosef, and C. Stringer, pp. 153-162. Cambridge, UK: McDonald Institute for Archaeological Research Monographs.

Soffer, O. 1985. *The Upper Paleolithic of the Central Russian Plain*. Orlando, FL: Academic Press.

——. 2001. "The Pyrotechnology of Performance Art: Moravian Venuses and Wolverines," in *Hunters of the Golden Age: The Mid-Upper Palaeolithic of Eurasia 30,000-20,000 BP*. Edited by W. Roebroeks, M. Mussi, J. Svoboda, and K. Fennema, pp. 259-275. Leiden: University of Leiden.

——. 2004. Recovering perishable technologies through use wear on tools: Preliminary evidence for Upper Paleolithic weaving and net making. *Current Anthropology* 45:407-412.

Solecki, R. 1970. Summary Report of the Columbia University Prehistoric Investigations in Lebanon, Season 1969. *Bulletin de la Musée de Beyrouth* 23:95-128.

Solecki, R. L., and R. L. Solecki. 1995. «The Mousterian Industries of Yabrud Shelter 1: A Reconsideration,» in *The Definition and Interpretation of Levallois Technology*. Edited by H. L. Dibble and O. Bar-Yosef, pp. 381-398. Madison, WI: Prehistory Press Monographs in World Archaeology No. 23.

Solecki, R. S. 1971. *Shanidar: The First Flower People.* New York: Alfred A. Knopf.

Solecki, R. S., and R. L. Solecki. 1993. "The pointed tools from the Mousterian occupations of Shanidar Cave, northern Iraq," in *The Paleolithic Prehistory of the Zagros-Taurus.* Edited by D. Olzewski and H. L. Dibble, pp. 119-146. Philadelphia, PA: University of Pennsylvania Museum (Monograph No. 83).

Stiner, M. C. 1993. Modern Human Origins -Faunal Perspectives. *Annual Review of Anthropology* 22:55-82.

—. 2006. *The Faunas of Hayonim Cave, Israel: A 200,000-Year Record of Paleolithic Diet, Demography, and Society.* Cambridge, MA: Peabody Museum Press, Harvard University.

Sullivan, A. P., III, and K. C. Rozen. 1985. Debitage Analysis and Archaeological Interpretation. *American Antiquity* 50:755-779.

Tchernov, E. 1988. "The Biogeographical History of the Southern Levant," in *The Zoogeography of Israel.* Edited by Y. Yom-Tov and E. Tchernov, pp. 401-409. Dordrecht: Junk.

—. 1998. "The Faunal Sequences of the Southwest Asian Middle Paleolithic in Relation to Hominid Dispersal Events," in *Neandertals and Modern Humans in Western Asia.* Edited by T. Akazawa, K. Aoki, and O. Bar-Yosef, pp. 77-90. New York: Plenum.

Theime, H. 1997. Lower Paleolithic Hunting Spears from Germany. *Nature* 385:807-810.

Toth, N., J. D. Clark, and G. Ligabue. 1992. The Last Stone Axe Makers. *Scientific American* 263:88-93.

Trinkaus, E. 2005. Early Modern Humans. *Annual Review of Anthropology* 34:207-230.

Turville-Petre, F. Editor. 1927. *Researches in Prehistoric Galilee: 1925-1926.* London: British School of Archaeology in Jerusalem.

Ungar, P. Editor. 2007. *Evolution of the Human Diet: The Known, the Unknown, and the Unknowable.* New York: Oxford University Press.

Valladas, H., J. L. Joron, G. Valladas, B. Arensburg, O. Bar-Yosef, A. Belfer-Cohen, P. Goldberg, H. Laville, L. Meignen, Y. Rak, E. Tchernov, A. M. Tillier, and B. Vandermeersch. 1987. Thermoluminscence dates for the Neanderthal burial site at Kebara in Israel. *Nature* 330:159-160.

Vandermeersch, B. 1966. L'industrie moustérienne de Larikba. *L'Anthropologie* 70:123-130.

Weinstein-Evron, M., G. Bar-Oz, Y. Zaidner, A. Tsatskin, D. Druck, N. Porat, and I. Hershkovitz. 2003. Introducing Misliya Cave, Mount Carmel, Israel: A New Continuous Lower/Middle Paleolithic Sequence in the Levant. *Eurasian Prehistory* 1:31-55.

White, J. P. 1968. "Ston Naip Bilong Tumbuna: The Living Stone Age in New Guinea," in *La Préhistoire: Problèmes et Tendances.* Edited by F. Bordes and D. de Sonneville-Bordes, pp. 511-516. Paris: CNRS.

White, T. D., B. Asfaw, D. DeGusta, H. Gilbert, G. Richards, G. Suwa, and F. C. Howell. 2003. Pleistocene Homo sapiens from Middle Awash, Ethiopia. *Nature* 423:742-747.

Whittaker, J. C. 2004. *American Flintknappers: Stone Age Art in the Age of Computers.* Austin: University of Texas Press.

Wilmsen, E. N. 1968. Functional Analysis of Flaked Stone Artifacts. *American Anthropologist* 33:151-161.

Wolpoff, M. H. 1989. "The Place of Neanderthals in Human Evolution," in *The Emergence of Modern Humans.* Edited by E. Trinkaus, pp. 97-141. New York: Cambridge University Press.

Wreschner, E. 1967. The Geula Caves, Mount Carmel: Excavations, Finds, and Summary. *Quaternaria* 9:69-90.

Zohary, M. 1962. *The Plant Life of Palestine: Israel and Jordan.* New York: Ronold.

—. 1973. *Geobotanical Foundations of the Middle East.* Stuttgart: Gustav Fischer Verlag.

www.ingramcontent.com/pod-product-compliance
Lightning Source LLC
Chambersburg PA
CBHW051306270326
41926CB00030B/4745